CROSSCURRENTS *Modern Critiques*

CROSSCURRENTS *Modern Critiques*
Harry T. Moore, *General Editor*

Richard Rees

Simone Weil

A SKETCH FOR A PORTRAIT

WITH A PREFACE BY

Harry T. Moore

Carbondale and Edwardsville

SOUTHERN ILLINOIS UNIVERSITY PRESS

PREFACE

SIR RICHARD REES has written about Simone Weil before, notably in Brave Men: A Study of D. H. Lawrence and Simone Weil (1958), which was published in London by Victor Gollancz and in the United States by the Southern Illinois University Press. And for the Oxford Press, Sir Richard has edited Simone Weil's Selected Essays, 1934–43 (1962), as well as Seventy Letters (1965), a translation of most of her available correspondence.

Besides this concentration on Simone Weil, Richard Rees has written a number of other books. One is an earlier volume in the present Crosscurrents/Modern Critiques series, George Orwell: Fugitive From the Camp of Victory (1962), published in London by Secker and Warburg in 1961. The same house also brought out his essays, For Love or Money (1960) and A Theory of My Time (1963), the former issued in America by the Southern Illinois University Press.

Richard Rees has also written many articles for leading British journals. He edited one of them, the Adelphi, from 1930 to 1936. A graduate of Cambridge, he became Secretary of that University's press in 1923, after experience in the diplomatic corps. He drove an ambulance for the Quakers in Spain at the time of the Civil War, and in 1939 he became Deputy Di-

rector of International Commission for Child Refu-
gees from Spain. At the time of the Second World
War, like so many pacifists, he joined the armed forces
and was assigned to one of the boats patrolling the
English Channel. He later received a commission, and
the French awarded him the Croix de Guerre.

These statistics provide a rather cold description of a
career. American college and university audiences that
have been fortunate enough to hear Richard Rees
lecture have found him a warm and lively figure—tall,
smiling through a small, salt-and-pepper beard, and
in all ways an excellent speaker. A number of the people he has met on these American tours have visited
his narrow, picturesque, three-story house (in English
terms, a two-storey house with a ground floor) in the
Chelsea district of London. A painting which shows
the view from the upper-floor parlor windows hangs
on our wall here in Illinois: besides depicting some
colorful Chelsea architecture, it shows, in its background, the tower of the church where Dickens was
married in 1836. This picture was painted by none
other than Richard Rees, who took up art for several
years after the Second World War and displayed his
work, which is far more than competent, at several
exhibitions. But in recent years writing has principally
engaged his interest; he finds that he hasn't time for
both painting and writing.

The results have been rewarding enough, both in
the satisfaction of accomplishment and in the friendly
public reception of the books. And I think the present
one the best of all. As I noted earlier, Richard Rees
has for a number of years devoted his attention to the
subject of Simone Weil, and he now speaks of her out
of a greater fund of knowledge than before. The edit-
ing of her Selected Essays and the Seventy Letters was
a fine preparation for this new book.

Like Simone Weil, Richard Rees's interests are both historical and philosophical; and if he is less overtly religious than she was, somewhat less mystic, he is nevertheless sensitively equipped to understand and expound her religious and mystic aspects. Further, he has a sympathetic admiration of her rather difficult personality, which he so marvelously presents in the first, or biographical, half of the present book. There is nothing that should be said here about this biographical sketch except to repeat that it is marvelous: the reader must enjoy it for himself. He should note, however, that Richard Rees is not blindly worshiping Simone Weil in these biographical passages; as he says toward the beginning of this book, he wants to avoid the extremes of presenting her as a dramatized "St. Joan of the Workshops" on the one hand or, on the other, as a sentimentalized "up-to-date blend of Hypatia and the Little Flower." It seems to me that he safely steers clear of these hazards. He views Simone Weil as a saint, taking the term from T. S. Eliot's reference to her; but Richard Rees shows that he knows how difficult a saint can be to have about the house. He is aware of occasional irascibility in her writing (as in some letters she wrote in 1937), but he also knows how fundamentally good she was; good is the only word, and he uses it.

Besides dealing with Simone Weil's "story," Richard Rees thoroughly examines her thinking. This has its roots in Plato, and yet she is a highly original philosopher. In her earlier writings she is concerned mostly with such problems as the duty of the individual and the nature of reality; and she becomes increasingly religious in her writing and thinking. Since she was so much the product of a time like our own — she was writing chiefly in the period between the two world wars, with conflict always threatening and at last breaking out—her problems are of acute interest today. Indeed, her last book, which was published in English in 1952 as The Need for Roots, has a definite historical-social content which is an important examination of the dilemma of modern man. Richard Rees, with his double interest in philosophy and history, is here particularly expert as an interpreter of Simone Weil's thought.

But he never really gets away from the personality of this young woman who actually killed herself by refusing to eat in England, while the people of her home country of France were being virtually starved by the Nazis occupying it. Hers was a strange but important martyrdom.

Like so many saints and martyrs, Simone Weil could often tell forth the truth in an oddly uncomfortable way, with what might be called saintly wit. Consider the piquant quotations, in the present volume, from her Notebooks, particularly this one about Jacob: "Isn't it the greatest possible disaster, when you are wrestling with God, not to be beaten?"

Her own life was a kind of protracted wrestling with God, and in her terms she would have thought of God as the victor.

Now we have this admirable book on Simone Weil, for which we should all be grateful to Sir Richard Rees. For it is a penetrating exploration, not only of Simone Weil, but of the times in which we exist.

HARRY T. MOORE

Southern Illinois University
September 11, 1965

CONTENTS

And because iniquity shall abound, the love of many shall wax cold. But he that shall endure to the end, the same shall be saved. — MATTHEW 24:12–13.

Dass man gerade nur denkt, wenn man das, worüber man denkt, nicht ausdenken kann. — GOETHE, Maximen und Reflexionen.

PART I

If the fool would persist in his folly, he would become wise. —WILLIAM BLAKE, *Proverbs of Hell.*

1 ENTRE DEUX GUERRES

WHEN I VISITED MUNICH in 1922, I was particularly struck by the number of doorplates bearing the legend *Nervenarzt*, nerve doctor. In that great centre of culture, still shabby and dilapidated after the great war, it seemed that out of every twenty apartments in the comparatively well-to-do quarters about ten were occupied by nerve doctors, psychoanalysts, or psychiatrists. One half of the population, apparently, was treating the nerves of the other half. It was rather like Park Avenue, New York, forty years later. But this was 1922, almost the beginning of the period known as *"entre deux guerres."*

The documentation for the history of Europe between the Treaty of Versailles and the outbreak of the Second World War in 1939 must be so voluminous that one wonders how historians will ever extract a coherent picture from it. But everyone who lived through the period has his own personal picture, and it is a useful exercise to try to imagine the picture as seen from someone else's angle of vision. Seen from England, mass unemployment is what would loom in the foreground for most people. In Germany, everything must have been coloured by a sense of national humiliation, resentment, and grievance. And in France, hardly less prostrated than Germany after four

years of massacre, the invasion of American tourists
profiting from the favourable exchange rate must have
seemed an outstanding phenomenon. More than one
large quarter of Paris became practically a colony of
artistic or dilettante or merely thirsty American expa-
triates.

In Germany people who could afford it nursed their
nerves and their complexes. In France "modern art"
began to boom. It would be sour to suggest that
psychoanalysis, surrealism, dadaism, and similar intellectual and artistic fashions of the 1920's were nothing
more than phenomena of decadence. But there is no
doubt that in some of their aspects they were symptoms of it; or if not of absolute decadence, at least of a
dangerously exhausted and disoriented state of mind.
Nations do not go through experiences like 1914–18
without some unhealthy aftereffects.

But war, of course, is also an agent of progress. The
neurotic demoralisation of large sections of the European public and the disillusionment of most of the
demobilised combatants were not the only results. A
great many anachronisms and hypocrisies were swept
away. A new spirit of optimism, both realistic and
idealistic, competed with cynicism and a sense of
insecurity in the minds of the young. The regime of
the warmongering "old men" was believed to have
passed away for ever. Much of this optimism was
light-headed, but nevertheless, and in spite of their
disastrous outcome, the years between 1918 and 1939
did in fact register considerable material progress and
some improvements in social morality in many countries. Even today, after a Second World War accompanied by atrocities on a scale that would have been
thought incredible at the beginning of the century, the
social atmosphere is in some ways freer, healthier,
more humane, and more pleasant in most of the

western countries than it was in 1900. But the world situation has altered beyond recognition, and in ways that hardly anybody foresaw during the *entre deux guerres*.

What had really happened, of course, as a result of 1914–18 was that Europe's world hegemony, which had been tottering for several decades, had finally collapsed. A new world was shaping itself, which would be dominated by new politico-economic units, of continental dimensions and organised *en bloc*, instead of consisting, like Europe, of an aggregation of independent sovereign States sharing a common culture and history but separated by economic rivalry and sentimental chauvinistic jealousy. (Probably the basic cause of the great war which hastened Europe's abdication was the reluctance of France and England to let Germany assume the powerful role in Europe for which she was obviously destined ever since Bismarck put her on the international political map.) By 1918 one of the new continental-scale world powers, the U.S.A., was fully formed and another, the U.S.S.R., was in the throes of birth. The collapse of Europe's hegemony was going very soon to involve the collapse of the European empires in Asia and Africa and, also, the radical reconstruction of the social and economic systems of the European countries.

The prospect of the end of imperialism abroad and the beginning of reconstruction at home was inspiring to the enlightened youth of every country. Kaisers, emperors, academies, dogmas, everything associated with the "old men" should be swept away. Oppressed workers and sweated coolies should come into their own. On the ruins of authoritarianism and paternalism a universal Liberty Hall should be built, whose foundation stone had already been laid in Russia in 1917. Freedom was in the ascendant—educational, artistic, sexual, moral, every kind of freedom; not the four beggarly freedoms of a later and sadder generation, but a thousand.

And some of it happened. But man proposes, God disposes, and the manner of its happening was ambiguous. Within a very few years the "Russian experiment" had developed into one of the most comprehensively authoritarian regimes, under one of the most tyrannical dictators, in the history of the world. And at almost the same time an authoritarian regime with a different label appeared in Italy, to be followed in 1933 by Hitler's dictatorship in Germany. The "old men" were back with a vengeance, and all the worse for being in reality vigorous gangsters in the prime of life. All one can say about England and France during this period is that they drifted helplessly towards the next war.

The modern world seems to lack whatever principle it is that discriminates between authority and tyranny and between liberty and license. And without such a principle it appears that one can only oscillate between the two lawless extremes.

The subject of this book is a French girl who came of age in 1930, the middle of the period I have been describing; and I have been trying to describe it from her angle of vision. Simone Weil was remarkable in many ways, one of them being that she thought for herself. She was a passionate patriot—indeed, one of the causes of her death was her despair at not being accepted for sabotage missions against the Germans in France in the Second World War—but she considered it unrealistic for twentieth-century France to strive for the rank of a world power in the material sense; a view which it required considerable independence of mind to hold, even on the political Left, in France in the 1930's. It required even more independence of mind, especially if one was Jewish, as she was, to maintain that the ultimate responsibility for Hitler's crimes must lie with the superstitious scientific culture which he, *in common with all modern people*, acquired in youth; and that the responsibility must therefore be shared by all who accept that culture. The capacity for independent thought, she believed, was already almost extinct in the modern world before the appearance of fascism; and "where irrational opinions hold the place of ideas, force is all-powerful. It is quite unfair to say, for example, that fascism annihilates free thought; in reality it is the lack of free thought which makes it possible to impose by force official doctrines entirely devoid of meaning." [1] She did not, however, believe that the erroneous view of the universe implicit in modern science is corrected by being combined with humanism. "In describing the universe solely as matter one grasps a fragment of truth. In describing it as a combination of matter and of specifically moral forces belonging to this world, on a level with nature, one falsifies everything." [2]

She also took an independent view of the new giant States whose influence had already begun to eclipse that of Europe. She saw the modern State apparatus, even in the small European States and *a fortiori* in the new continental-scale models, as a form of social idol, as indeed the only powerful ersatz divinity, in a world that had lost the true sense of authority. She thought that State Socialism, of the kind which modern political and economic trends make ultimately inevitable everywhere, achieves the opposite of what socialism professes to do. It may sometimes be efficient in organising mass production and consumption, but so far from liberating the proletariat, it reduces the whole

of society to the proletarian condition. This phenomenon she regarded as the fatal legacy to the world of the
Roman Empire.

I have collected together in tabloid form a few of
Simone Weil's more provocative opinions, which will
be much more intelligible when they emerge later
within the context of the rest of her work. My purpose
in placing them here is to emphasise that she was an
unorthodox and challenging thinker, and not the
anodyne purveyor of "golden thoughts" that she is
sometimes supposed to be. The best brief description
of her paradoxical temperament is T. S. Eliot's preface
to *The Need for Roots*, where he describes her as
"more truly a lover of order and hierarchy than most of
those who call themselves Conservative, and more
truly a lover of the people than most of those who call
themselves Socialist."

That her sympathies and antipathies were sometimes intemperate and her affirmations too extreme
cannot be denied. But she was only thirty-four when
she died, and at that early age she was already phe-
nomenal among the intellectuals of her period in the
range and the relative maturity of her thought. Unique
and unclassifiable as a thinker, she was neither a
reactionary nor a progressive. She was something
altogether exceptional—a great soul and a brilliant
mind, as Eliot expresses it, "with a kind of genius akin
to that of the saints."

But these are dangerous words. An attribution of
saintliness is almost a kiss of death in an enlightened
age like our own, in which barbarous words like good
and evil are falling into disuse. In place of evil we now
have maladjustment and antisocial or reactionary
complexes, and in place of good we have maturity and
successful social adaptation. I shall try, however, in
these pages to avoid quarrelling about words (mature

cancer? well-adjusted yes-man?); and as regards saintliness I shall follow George Orwell's advice that saints
should always be held guilty until their innocence has
been proved—or, in modern language, that eccentric
behaviour should always be attributed to immaturity
or maladjustment, unless it can be shown to result
from a more perfect maturity and a finer adjustment
than the normal.

THERE IS A CHARACTER in a French novel,[1] reputed to be a skit on Simone Weil, who is always limping. The reason is that she has bought ill-fitting shoes from an impoverished friend, as a way of giving her money. Simone Weil was a person about whom stories of that kind would be likely to be told. She travelled with awkward parcels and bags. (One of her friends described her luggage as "improbable.") She spilled boiling oil over herself while cooking at the front in the Spanish Civil War. She dressed sometimes worse than plainly and was indifferent to her appearance. Apart from close friends, she seems to have been more at home with her pupils (she taught at girls' Lycées) and with workmen (she worked in factories) than with her fellow intellectuals. One of the latter [2] has written that she spoke in a superior, drawling, *"gnan-gnan"* voice, which sounds like a French equivalent of the Cambridge and Bloomsbury accent of the 1920's. And people sometimes found her difficult.

When she died in England during the Second World War, the half dozen French exiles at her funeral saw one other mourner, an impoverished-looking Englishwoman in shabby wartime Sunday best, who hung back until the last moment but finally came to the graveside and gazed in, smiling very sadly and tenderly, then threw in a tricolour bunch of flowers, white, blue, and red, and walked away very quickly to the station.[3] This was the London landlady, a poor widow with two small children, with whom Simone Weil had lodged for three months, until her last illness. She had travelled from London to Ashford to attend the funeral. She had not found her lodger difficult.

In writing about Simone Weil it seems inevitable to begin with a discussion of her personality; but it is also ironic, because she regarded personality as an obstacle to all the highest human achievements, and her essay on the human personality,[4] which is in fact about the destruction of personality, is one of the most important and least understood, and sometimes when understood one of the most disliked, of all her essays.

Her short life of thirty-four years was sufficiently eventful and striking to justify a book for its own sake; but her essays, many of which did not appear until after her death, and her posthumously published notebooks contain material which, although not more than moderately voluminous, is of a profundity and richness and variety to which it would require a very exceptional biographer and critic to do justice. Unfortunately, on the other hand, it is all too easy for any biographer to dramatise her as a sort of St. Joan of the Workshops or to sentimentalise her as an up-to-date blend of Hypatia and the Little Flower. But these two pitfalls I shall at least avoid because I believe that the attempt to understand her thought is impeded by an overintense concern with the impressive and touching and picturesque traits of her career—though it is to be hoped, of course, that a full account of it will appear some day, as part of a complete and adequate presentation of her ideas.* In this short volume I can do no more than indicate what appear to me to be the main outlines of her thought and set them within the framework of a brief biographical sketch.

Simone Weil was the second child and only daughter of Dr. Bernard Weil and his wife, Selma. Dr. Weil was a distinguished Paris physician and both he and his wife were freethinking Jews. They brought their children up without religious instruction but in an atmosphere of high and eclectic moral culture. Simone was born in Paris on February 3, 1909, three years after her brother, André. In his early years André Weil already showed extraordinary promise of mathematical ability; and both he and his sister were to become in due course exceptionally brilliant students at the Ecole Normale Supérieure, which is the summit of the French educational system. To be received at the Normale is to be part of the cream of the French intellect of one's generation.

Judging by photographs, she was a gay and pretty child, but beneath the surface her temperament must have been strangely serious and profound. She was only five when the First World War broke out, but she put unusual determination into such fairly normal actions as sacrificing her sugar for the soldiers at the front. And we have her own word for it that at the age of nine, when the war ended, she was mature enough to feel outraged at the humiliations inflicted upon Germany and revolted by French jingoism. "I suffer more," she wrote years later to Georges Bernanos,

* The fullest presentation so far, in both respects, is Jacques Cabaud's *Simone Weil* (New York: Appleton-Century-Crofts, 1965). There is also a good short account of her thought in François Heidsieck's study in the series *Philosophes de tous les temps* (Paris: Seghers, 1965).

"from the humiliations inflicted by my country than from those inflicted on her."

Another significant trait which she remembered from her childhood was her discouragement, and perhaps envy, at the intellectual precocity of her brother. The passage referring to this in her long letter to Father Perrin in 1942 [5] reveals so much of her character and her thought that a detailed commentary on it will make the best possible introduction to both.

> At the age of fourteen I fell into one of those fits of bottomless despair which come with adolescence; and I seriously thought of dying, because of the mediocrity of my natural faculties. The extraordinary gifts of my brother, who had a childhood and youth comparable to those of Pascal, made me forcibly aware of this. What I minded was not the lack of external successes but the having no hope of access to that transcendent realm where only the truly great can enter and where truth dwells. I felt it better to die than to live without truth.

Simone Weil always means precisely and literally what she says. When she said that the humiliations inflicted on Germany made her suffer, she meant that at the age of nine she really suffered. In fact, for all the rest of her life the knowledge that weakness is almost always and almost everywhere oppressed by strength was literal torture to her. In the same way when she says that at the age of fourteen death seemed to her preferable to life without truth she means exactly that. And when she speaks about the mediocrity of her natural faculties she believes, however mistakenly, that it is true. And indeed it may be true that her natural faculties did not include any very special or remarkable talents, but only a brilliant and powerful intellect which, like all intellect, can be compared to a machine. Intellect can help a man to develop his talents, but it is not itself a talent. Simone Weil possessed a good ear for poetry and music and a gift for languages, but her own poetry seems to be overburdened with erudition. What she possessed was not talent; it was genius, which is not, as she defines it, a natural faculty. As we shall see, some of her most valuable work is concerned with the definition of genius. The letter continues:

> After months of inner darkness I gained, suddenly and for ever, the certainty that any human being at all, even if his natural faculties are almost nil, finds his way into that realm of truth which is reserved for genius, if only he longs for truth and makes a perpetual effort of attention so as to reach it. In this way he too becomes a genius, even though, for want of talent, no genius is externally visible.

Once again, we can be quite certain that that is exactly what Simone Weil believed when she was fourteen, and that she immediately began to make the effort of attention which she conceived to be necessary, and that she continued it "perpetually." Now, these are not the thoughts and this is not the behaviour of a normal little girl. But in order to decide in what sense her behaviour was abnormal, it needs to be tested by the highest standards. By Blake's, for example, when he said that "if the fool would persist in his folly he would become wise." These words of Blake might well serve as a text for a great part of Simone Weil's work, and more particularly for her psychological ideas. At the centre of her system she puts desire; and it is through repeated disillusionments, through persistence in folly, that we can learn what the real object of our desire is. But most of us fail to persevere. In the end, we settle for an illusion, pretending to ourselves that we believe it is real. She began by paying a severe price for her own persistence, as the next passage of the letter shows.

> *Later on, when headaches weighed upon the few faculties I possess and caused a paralysis which I was quick to suppose was probably incurable, it was this same certainty* [that truth is accessible to everyone] *that made me persevere through ten years of efforts of attention which were practically unsupported by any hope of results.*

The ten years referred to are her twenty-first to her thirty-first (1930–40),[6] and it is more than surprising to discover what she actually did during those ten years of "paralysed" faculties. I have never heard any satisfactory explanation of the headaches, but they may have originated from the strain of working for her *agrégation* at the Ecole Normale, which she passed brilliantly in 1931. She herself describes them as "pain around the central point of the nervous system" and says that it "persists during sleep and has never stopped for a second."[7] After 1940, when she had only three years to live, they appear to have eased a little, but even at their worst they never prevented her from undertaking, and hardly ever seem to have interrupted her in, physical and intellectual labour which might have strained the most powerful physique.

To me it seems that the headaches could be explained as part of the torment she suffered from the fact of universal injustice. At any rate, it is obvious that they were psychosomatic, whatever that may mean, and she herself anticipates the modish label by describing the "central point of the nervous system" as "the meeting place of soul and body." But this does not take us much further unless we know her definition of soul, which must be left until later. The material fact is that she felt pain, and sometimes almost disabling pain, for a period of at least ten years. So her activities during those years, which cover about 80 per cent of her adult life, provide a good test of her method of making efforts of attention even when almost unsupported by any hope of results. They can be summarised as follows.

She taught successively at the Lycées of Le Puy, Auxerre, Roanne, Bourges, and St Quentin; she spent the summer of 1932 in Berlin, studying the political situation just before Hitler's accession to power; she worked for nine months (1934/35) as an unskilled operative in factories in the Paris region; she spent two months of 1936 at the front in the Spanish Civil War; she travelled in Portugal, Switzerland, and Italy; and she wrote the greater part of the material that was to fill fourteen posthumous volumes and possibly others still to come. During the remaining three years of her life, still afflicted by headaches though less acutely, she was to work as an agricultural labourer, do some of her most important writing, and cross the Atlantic twice in wartime.

To return to her letter:

> Under the name of truth I included also beauty, virtue and every kind of good, so that for me it was a question of a relation between grace and desire. The certainty I had received was that when one desires bread one does not receive stones. But in those days I had not read the Gospel.

Since she had not read the Gospel at the age of fourteen, she probably did not use the word grace at that time when formulating her idea. The appearance of simplicity in this passage is very deceptive. She is saying that when she envied her brother his access to the realm of truth she conceived truth as including every good that a human being can desire. So the words "when one desires bread one does not receive stones" mean, in addition to their obvious meaning, that when one desires truth one is not satisfied with

illusions. One would "receive stones" only too will-
ingly if they satisfied one's hunger, but they do not.
"At the centre of the human heart," she wrote elsewhere, "is the longing for an absolute good, a longing
which is always there and is never appeased by any
object in this world"; [8] and in another place: "At the
bottom of the heart of every human being, from
earliest infancy until the tomb, there is something that
goes on indomitably expecting, in the teeth of all
experience of crimes committed, suffered and witnessed, that good and not evil will be done to him. It
is this above all that is sacred in every human being. . . . and even in the most corrupt of men it
remains from earliest infancy perfectly intact and
totally innocent." [9] What she meant by bread was the
absolute good, for which no object in this world can be
a substitute. She believed that it comes to us in
response to our attention to it. But she gave the word
attention a particular meaning. It is not an effort
involving tension of the will or the muscles, neither is
it an inert passivity. It is one of her basic psychological terms, and we shall return to it later.

The next passage of the letter is related to another of
her psychological ideas—*l'imagination combleuse de
vides:* that the uncontrolled imagination is always
prone to the vice of day-dreaming, the imaginary filling
up of emotional voids. But to allow desire to drain
itself into wish fulfilments is to degrade it.

> *Just as I was certain that desire possesses an efficacy in
> itself in this sphere of spiritual good in all its forms, so I
> thought I could be certain that it has no efficacy in any
> other.*

So at the age of fourteen she became convinced that
the only things that come to us in response to our
desire are spiritual goods; and she also believed that

nothing else is worth desiring. One might think that a girl of fourteen whose mind worked in this way would have thoughts of becoming a nun. But there are obvious reasons why no such idea could have occurred to Simone Weil. In the first place, she had no religion but was for many years a Stoic and an agnostic; and in the second place, even if she had had a religious upbringing she would still undoubtedly have considered love and justice between men to be among the highest spiritual goods and would have found her own spiritual good in trying to uphold them in the world. Her political evolution would have been exactly the same as it in fact was.

IN HER LETTER to Father Perrin, Simone Weil also touches on another aspect of adolescence. At the age of sixteen she experienced "several months of the emotional unrest natural to adolescence," but at the end of that time "the idea of purity" took possession of her. "This idea came to me while I was contemplating a mountain landscape and imposed itself on me little by little in an irresistible manner." This must have been in 1925, and it does not seem to imply anything like a permanent vow of chastity. More likely, in view of the way of life of intellectual teen-agers at that time, it was a rejection of current standards of sexual morality. She specifically states that her notion of purity corresponded exactly to the Christian one.

She does not often write about herself, but when she does there is something painful in the picture one gets of an unmitigated seriousness, an unvarying grave intensity. It seems all work and no play, and still less any humour. But her other writings do not altogether bear this out, nor do her photographs, nor do the reminiscences of her friends. In her teens she looks rather intense, but her later photographs nearly always show her with a serene and gentle expression, though they show that a plain neatness was the most she even aimed at in her appearance. However, her words about

falling in love, written at the age of twenty-six to a
pupil, do not suggest that at any given moment she
categorically ruled it out; but they are written in her
gravest didactic vein.

> Love is a serious thing; and it often means pledging
> one's own life and also that of another human being, for
> ever. Indeed, it always means that, unless one of the two
> treats the other as a plaything; and in that case, which is
> a very common one, love is something odious. In the
> end, you see, the essential point in love is this: that one
> human being feels a vital need of another human
> being—a need which is or is not reciprocal and is or is
> not enduring, as the case may be. Consequently, the
> problem arises of reconciling this need with freedom,
> and it is a problem with which men have struggled from
> time immemorial. . . . I can tell you that when, at your
> age, and later on too, I was tempted to try to get to know
> love, I decided not to—telling myself it was better not to
> commit my life in a direction impossible to foresee until
> I was sufficiently mature to know what, in a general way,
> I wish from life and what I expect from it.[1]

In 1941, when she worked in a vineyard near the
Rhône, she was proud when the farmer told her she
would make a fit wife for a peasant.[2]

As regards humour, there is no doubt that she could
be wryly and sardonically witty, though the flashes are
rare in her books. She is, so far as I know, the only
writer who has pointed out that Marx's famous dictum
might well be reworded: Revolution is the people's
opium; and there is some brisk ridicule of pragmatism
in *The Need for Roots*.

> In Bergson, religious faith is presented like a "Pink pill"
> of a superior kind, which imparts a prodigious amount
> of vitality. The same thing applies to the historical
> argument, which consists in saying: "Look what a miser-
> able lot men were before Christ. Christ came, and see

how men, in spite of their backslidings, afterwards became, on the whole a good lot!" That is absolutely contrary to the truth. But even if it were true, it reduces apologetics to the level of advertisements for pharmaceutical products, which describe the state of the patient before and after.[3]

Anyone who reads the letters she wrote from Italy in 1937 [4] will understand why some of her friends and relations are bewildered when critics accuse her—not without some apparent justification—of a masochistic preoccupation with pain and suffering. It is true that in these letters she never loses sight of the tragic farce by which the fate of the most civilised, most generous, and least aggressive people in the world got into the hands of hysterical fascist bravoes. Nevertheless the letters give, on the whole, a picture of tireless, joyful energy. She notices and admires and enjoys talking to the handsome young conscripts and peasants; she crams the days full with art galleries, churches, concerts, plays, films, and meals at cheap cafés and suburban *trattorie*. In Rome, she praises the Sistine choir, the Greek statues, the wine, and the ice cream. She makes friends everywhere, on trains and boats and in remote villages. She reads the *Fioretti*, Galileo, Machiavelli, and the poems of Michelangelo and Lorenzo de'Medici; and after reading Giraudoux's *Electre* she exclaims: "Why have I not the *n* existences I need, in order to devote one of them to the theatre!"

And in a different way her letters to her brother in 1940 are equally striking. Few people in France can have suffered more mental distress than she did at the events of that year; but this did not prevent her from engaging in a long philosophical and historical correspondence about Greek, Egyptian, and Babylonian mathematics.[5] These letters remind one of Archimedes at the fall of Syracuse. On the other hand, there is a piece of reliable gossip from the Spanish Civil War which reveals her in quite a frivolous light. She was treated for her burns at the hospital at Sitges, and her parents managed to get into Spain to visit her. To her father's professional eye the treatment seemed unsatisfactory, and he was able, assisted probably by some feud in the hospital which anyone who was in Spain in those days can easily imagine, to get her removed. But as she was being carried, accompanied by the inevitable group of loungers, across the hospital courtyard, the doctor discovered what was happening and called from a window: "What are you doing with my patient? Stop! I must come down and take her temperature." At this point it was noticed that the patient was shaking with laughter.

> "What is the matter with you? Really, Simone, this hardly seems the time—"
> "It isn't the place either, the way they take temperatures here!"

Between 1931, when she took up her first teaching appointment at the Lycée for girls at Le Puy, and her return from the Spanish Civil War at the end of 1936, Simone Weil appears to have been absorbed in labour problems and politics. But one of her letters is enough to prove that this did not interfere with her concern for her pupils. Finding that the members of her philosophy class had rudimentary ideas, or none at all, about the relationship between the different sciences, she offered to give a series of supplementary lectures on the history of science, which were attended voluntarily in their spare time by the whole class.

> I gave them a rapid sketch of the development of mathematics, taking as central theme the duality: continuous versus discontinuous, and describing it as the

attempt to deal with the continuous by means of the discontinuous, measurement itself being the first step. I told them the history of Greek science: similar triangles (Thales and the Pyramids)—Pythagoras' theorem—discovery of incommensurables and the crisis it provoked—solution of the crisis by Eudoxus' theory of proportions—discovery of conics, *as sections of the cone*—method of exhaustion—and of the geometry of early modern times (algebra—analytic geometry—principle of the differential and integral calculus). I explained to them—as no one had troubled to do—how the infinitesimal calculus was the condition for the application of mathematics to physics and consequently for the contemporary efflorescence of physics. All this was followed by all of them, even those most ignorant in science, with passionate interest.[6]

Nevertheless, somewhere inside the twenty-two-year-old lecturer on philosophy and the history of science there was still the little girl of fourteen, thirsting for the truth, the whole truth and nothing but the truth. She now conceived it in terms of "contact with real life." And real life was not the sheltered life of the intellectual Parisian bourgeoisie or of provincial Lycées; it was the life of the great anonymous mass of the unprivileged, those who throughout history have borne the real burden of life as slaves, serfs, soldiers, farmers, masons, craftsmen, labourers, or proletarian industrial workers. But for all her youth and enthusiasm there was no sentimental optimism in her approach to working-class life. It is true that she believed that a factory ought to be "a place where one makes a hard and painful, but nevertheless joyful, contact with real life";[7] but when, after two years of teaching, she went, taking her headaches with her, to work in an electrical factory in Paris, she was fully prepared to find that the joy was missing. Her first step, in 1932, had been to join a study circle organised in connection with the magazine *Révolution prolétarienne* at the Labour Exchange at St Etienne, some forty miles from Le Puy, and she went over once a week or more all the time she was at Le Puy and later, in 1933, when she was teaching at Roanne.

In this way she made contact with the leading trade unionists of the district and more particularly with those of the miners' federation. During a strike she limited her expenses to the amount of the miners' unemployment pay, giving the surplus to the miners' funds and for the purchase of books for political study circles. She also took part in a deputation, was attacked in the local press, and caused embarrassment to her official superiors. But none of this, naturally, affected her popularity with her pupils, whatever their parents may have felt about it.

In the period 1932–34 she wrote two important political essays. The first, "Prospects" [8] appeared in *Révolution prolétarienne* but the second, a much longer essay, "Reflections concerning the Causes of Liberty and Social Oppression," [9] which her former teacher, Alain, described as *"de première grandeur,"* was not published until after her death. She also wrote, for *L'Ecole émancipée*, a series of articles from Berlin, where she spent the summer vacation of 1932, lodging in the house of a Communist worker. The Berlin articles give a depressingly clearheaded analysis of the situation in the period just before Hitler's victory, and also a few pungent topical observations. One of these observations concerns the contagiousness of the Nazi ideology, "notably with the Communists":

> Recently the Nazis were denouncing the fact that "a Marxist Jewess" (Clara Zetkin) would be president when the Reichstag reassembled. To which the *Welt am Abend* (official Communist newspaper) replied: "In the first place, Clara Zetkin is not Jewish. And in the second place, it would make no difference if she were.

Rosa Luxemburg, *although a Jewess,* was an altogether *ehrliche Person* (honourable person)!" [10]

It was not only this kind of psychological vice, however, but the entire German political, economic, and social situation which convinced her of the possibility of what was in fact to happen some six years later—a Nazi-Soviet pact.

But in spite of the sober and even sombre realism of the political analyses she wrote from Germany, there is one conventional slogan which keeps recurring: workers' control. "At the beginning of a revolutionary period," she says, "the immediate objective of the workers" should be workers' control of production. And this motif runs through the whole series of articles. One might think here that she was talking with the same facile optimism as so many of the young, idealistic intellectuals of the 1930's, who took the possibility of workers' control of industry for granted. Government by soviets or workers' councils was on everybody's lips, but usually without the slightest attempt to conceive how it could function in practice. But when we turn from Simone Weil's reports from Germany to the article she wrote for *Révolution prolétarienne* and to the long essay on the causes of liberty and oppression we find that there was nothing conventional or facile in her approach to this subject, and that it was for her the crux of the whole social problem.

As nearly as I can summarise it, the argument of both the article and the essay is as follows: Liberty is not the mere absence of all necessity; to conceive it so is to make it meaningless.

True liberty is not defined by a relationship between desire and its satisfaction, but by a relationship between thought and action; the absolutely free man would be he whose every action proceeded from a preliminary judgment concerning the end which he set himself and the sequence of means suitable for attaining this end.[11]

Thus there is oppression wherever men work as passive instruments carrying out ideas in which they do not participate. This is what Marx called the "degrading division of labour into intellectual and manual labour."

A team of workers on a production-line under the eye of a foreman is a sorry sight, whereas it is a fine sight to see a handful of workmen in the building trade, checked by some difficulty, ponder the problem each for himself, make various suggestions for dealing with it, and then apply unanimously the method conceived by one of them, who may or may not have any official authority over the remainder. At such moments the image of a free community appears almost in its purity.[12]

But the organisation of industry in the twentieth century, whether under a communist, a fascist, or a so-called democratic regime, involves specialisation and division of labour to such an extent that not only manual workers but technicians and scientists also are victims of "the degrading division of labour."

the technicians are ignorant of the theoretical basis of the knowledge which they employ. The scientists in their turn not only remain out of touch with technical problems but in addition are entirely cut off from that over-all vision which is the very essence of theoretical culture. One could count on one's fingers the number of scientists in the entire world who have a general idea of the history and development of their own particular science; there is not one who is really competent as regards sciences other than his own. As science forms an indivisible whole, one may say that there are no longer, strictly speaking, any scientists, but only drudges doing scientific work, cogs in a mechanism which their minds cannot embrace as a whole. . . . In such a situation, there is one function which takes on a supreme importance, namely, that which consists simply in coordinating; we may call it the administrative or bureaucratic function.[13]

Remembering that Simone Weil defines oppression as being forced to work as a passive instrument of designs one neither understands nor even knows, it follows that a bureaucratic State is still an oppressive State, no matter how much it raises the standard of living of its subjects. Moreover, "the degrading division of labour into intellectual and manual labour" is equally degrading for intellectual and manual workers alike. Ideally speaking, she says, the most fully human civilisation would be that which had manual labour as its pivot, that in which "manual labour constituted the supreme value." Before she worked in factories Simone Weil had already done some hard labour on the land, and she was speaking from experience when she added to the words I have just quoted.

Even in these days, so-called disinterested activities, such as sport or art or even thought, perhaps do not succeed in giving the equivalent of what one experiences in getting directly to grips with the world by means of non-mechanised labour. Rimbaud complained that "we are not in the world" and that "true life is absent." In those moments of incomparable joy and fullness we know by flashes that true life *is* present, we feel with our whole being that the world exists and that we are in the world.[14]

D. H. Lawrence said exactly the same.

Incomplete though it is, this outline of Simone Weil's thought in 1932–34, before she decided to experience

for herself the life of an unskilled factory hand, will
have made it clear why she made workers' control the
touchstone for judging socialist policy. Bureaucratic
Russian communism, even apart from the terrorism of
the Stalin regime, failed her test as completely as the
western bureaucratic regimes.

> Every human group that exercises power does so, not in
> such a way as to bring happiness to those who are
> subject to it, but in such a way as to increase that power.
> To do so is a matter of life and death for any form of
> domination whatsoever. As long as production remained
> at a primitive stage of development, the question of
> power was decided by armed force. Economic changes
> transferred it to the plane of production itself; it was in
> this way that the capitalist system came into
> being. . . . Capitalism is only a system for exploiting
> productive work. In every sphere of activity, except for
> the proletariat's struggle for emancipation, it has given
> full scope to initiative, free enquiry, invention, and
> genius. On the other hand, the bureaucratic machine,
> which excludes all judgement and all genius, tends, by
> its very structure, to concentrate all powers in itself.
> Therefore it threatens the existence even of such values
> as still survive for us in the bourgeois regime. . . .
>
> Are we really threatened with subjection to such a
> system? We are perhaps more than threatened; it seems
> as though we could see it taking shape before our
> eyes.[15]

Once again, she is not thinking only of Russia or
Nazi Germany; she is thinking of all highly indus-
trialised modern States. And she judges them to be
oppressive not only because of the factory system, the
specialisation and rationalisation which kill the
workers' initiative, but also because of the intellectual
atmosphere which kills independence of mind. Thus it
is rather misleading that what she wrote about labour
conditions after she had spent a year working in

factories is so very largely concerned with the monotony and passivity of the life of the unskilled worker.
She discussed this point at great length with two
well-disposed industrialists, and she had great difficulty
in convincing them that her picture of factory conditions was not coloured by her own personal unsuit-
ability for monotonous and unskilled work. And there
is no doubt that they were right in thinking that many
people can perform monotonous and mindless tasks
without the irritation that she felt, and that some
people even prefer them to tasks calling for initiative
and thought. But this is to miss her whole point. Her
point is that a life-time spent in mindless drudgery is
degrading, and that if people are degraded to the point
where they actually prefer to work mindlessly, then our
civilisation is a failure. In the much-heralded future
age of leisure, if people do mindless work for short
hours in comfortable conditions, they will still only be
contented sheep, instead of lean and hungry ones.
Simone Weil's point is that men are not sheep—a
point which will, of course, be disputed by politicians
and cynics.

She was, in any case, sceptical about the age of
leisure. "Aristotle admitted that there would no longer
be anything to stand in the way of the abolition of
slavery if it were possible to have the indispensable
work done by 'mechanical slaves,' and when Marx
attempted to forecast the future of the human species,
all he did was to take up this idea and develop it"; [16]
but a state of affairs in which men could have as much
enjoyment and as little fatigue as they liked could exist
nowhere except in science fiction. Nor is it a utopia on
which we need waste any regret.

> One has only to bear in mind the frailty of human
> nature to understand that a life from which the very
> notion of work had practically disappeared would be

given over to the passions and perhaps to madness; there is no self-mastery without discipline, and there is no other source of discipline for man than the effort imposed by external obstacles. A nation of idlers could no doubt amuse itself by setting up obstacles, by exerting itself in science, art, and sport; but exertions that arise out of pure whim do not provide men with the means of controlling their whims. . . . The only freedom one can ascribe to the Golden Age is that which little children would enjoy if their parents imposed no rules on them; it is really only an unconditional surrender to caprice. The human body can never in any case be free from dependence upon the mighty universe that enfolds it; even if man ceased to be subjected to material objects and to other men by needs and dangers, he would be only the more enslaved to them by emotions perpetually travailing in his depths, from which no regular occupation would any longer protect him.[17]

Although these ideas run counter to the fashionable permissive outlook in psychology and education, they are none the less unanswerable. But they can lead to two different conclusions. Namely, the two conclusions that were debated between Ivan and Alyosha Karamazov. Supposing—to use Simone Weil's image, which is also used, for the opposite purpose, by Ivan's Grand Inquisitor—that men *are* no more than little children, for whom the Golden Age would mean surrendering to their caprices under the watchful eye of indulgent parents? In that case, the Grand Inquisitor's solution is the best: "In their leisure hours we shall make their life like a child's game, with children's songs and innocent dance. Oh, we shall allow them even sin, and they will love us like children because we allow them to sin . . . thousands of millions of happy babes." [18]

Who is right—Alyosha and Simone Weil, or Ivan and the Grand Inquisitor? In the end one must choose between two ideas of liberty. The free man is either the man who can obtain pleasure without effort, or he is the man "whose every action proceeds from a preliminary judgement concerning the end which he sets himself and the sequence of means suitable for attaining this end." Or, to put it in another way:

> Living man can never cease to be hemmed in on all sides by an absolutely inflexible necessity; but since he is able to think, he has the choice between reacting blindly to the spur with which necessity pricks him on from outside, or else adapting himself to the inner representation of it which he forms in his own mind; and it is in this that the difference between slavery and freedom consists.[19]

Simone Weil championed freedom, which may be the act of a fool; but she was prepared, as we shall see, to persist in her folly to the uttermost extreme.

BY 1934, her first-hand experience in France and Germany and her reading of the situation in Russia and America had convinced Simone Weil that without "a methodical cooperation between all, both strong and weak, with a view to progressively decentralising social life"—a cooperation which it would, of course, be absurd to hope for—there was no way of stopping the blind and universal trend towards an increasing centralisation "until the machine suddenly jams and flies into pieces." [1] Whether this occurs within centuries or within decades, it is, in her view, ultimately inevitable.

> In such a situation, what can those do who still persist, in spite of and against everything, in honouring human dignity? Nothing, except endeavour to introduce a little play into the cogs of the machine that is grinding us down; seize every opportunity of awakening a little thought wherever they are able.[2]

Such an endeavour calls not only for knowledge but also for thorough personal experience of the machine. As a first step she obtained, in 1934, a year's leave "for private study" and, thanks to Auguste Detoeuf, an industrialist and a very remarkable man, to whom she had been given an introduction, she was hired as an unskilled hand at the Alsthom electrical works in

Paris. She took a room at 228 rue Lecourbe, near the factory, and lived, or existed, on her pay. No one in the workshops knew that she was an *agrégée* of the Normale and a lecturer in philosophy, and apart from one or two rare perceptive individuals whom she mentions in her factory diary no one seems to have noticed anything unusual about her.

She spent nine shattering months at the Alsthom and two other factories (the Forges de Basse-Indre and Renault's) and emerged in August, 1935, feeling that she was marked for ever with the brand of slavery. But, for all her political pessimism, she never quite despaired. She could still write at the end of her life, in 1943, that the one original idea of our civilisation, the *only* one that we have not borrowed from the Greeks, is the idea of the spirituality of labour. (In 1935 she would probably have used the word 'dignity' rather than 'spirituality.') In this respect, she said, "Plato himself was only a forerunner: the Greeks knew art and sport, but not labour." [3] Presentiments of this vocation of realising the spirituality of labour can be found "in Rousseau, George Sand, Tolstoy, Proudhon and Marx, in papal encyclicals and elsewhere," [4] and it is because we have been unequal to our vocation that we have fallen into the totalitarian abyss. And she asks herself with anguish if it is perhaps still not too late to redeem ourselves.

The spirituality of labour is a difficult expression, and it would hardly be too much to say that the whole of Simone Weil's work is an attempt to elucidate it. There is more than one vocabulary for the purpose, and towards the end of her life she tended to use the religious one, in which alone it can be completely expressed — saying that the purpose of all work is to bring man into contact with God, or the supernatural, and that physical labour is, or rather could be, specially privileged in that it is the most direct method. But in 1935, when she emerged from the Renault factory feeling like a slave, she had not yet acquired a religious vocabulary. There was nothing noticeably servile, however, about the language in which she continued to champion the workers and criticise the employers.

She was appointed to the Lycée at Bourges, where she soon made contact with B——, the manager of a local factory producing stoves. This Monsieur B—— must have been an extremely well-intentioned man. He had started a factory magazine, *Entre Nous*, by which he hoped to promote understanding between workers and management. Simone Weil not only had many interviews with him but also, between January and June, 1936, wrote him letters totalling some twelve thousand words describing, from her previous year's experience, the frustrations and indignities of factory labour; making suggestions; and even discussing the possibility of enrolling as an operative in his factory, in order to cooperate with him from below in improving the conditions of work. There was also a plan for her to edit anonymously a section of *Entre Nous* in which the workers would be encouraged to write about their work and ventilate their grievances. I think it says a good deal for B—— that their relationship continued harmoniously for as long as six months. He began, however, by rejecting her first article for *Entre Nous* on the ground that it was an incitement to class feeling. It was in fact a very moving appeal to the workers to collaborate with her in enlightening the management about the real problems of a worker's life. It began, however, with the words: "Dear unknown friends, who are toiling (*qui peinez*) in the Rosières workshops," and although it said nothing abusive or unfair about the management it was couched in terms which B—— could hardly fail to find ominous.[5] Later he published an article summarising the story of *Antigone* which she sent him with the ironic hope that "he would not find Sophocles subversive." She intended to write a series of similar articles on Greek literature for working-class readers, whom she considered more capable of really understanding it, and more worthy of it, than bourgeois intellectuals.

But her relations with B—— came to an abrupt end in June, through her attitude toward the victory of the workers in the stay-in strikes in Paris—when the employers were locked out and the workers occupied the factories for several days. She wrote to B—— on June 10, postponing a visit to his factory for fear he might feel she was abusing his hospitality if she congratulated his workers on the victory of their Paris comrades and sympathised with "their relief at being for once given way to by those who dominate them." Bitterly offended, B—— sent a brief, stinging reply and broke off relations. It is not known how he reacted to her reply to his snub, in which she said, among other things, that her joy was not only on behalf of the workers but also on behalf of the employers.

> I am not thinking now of their material interests—it may be that the results of the strike will be disastrous in the end for the material interests of both sides, one cannot tell—but of their moral interests, the good of their souls. I think it is good for the oppressed to have been able to assert their existence for a few days and lift their heads and impose their will and obtain some advantages which they do not owe to a condescending generosity. And I think it is equally good for the bosses—for the good of their souls—to have been obliged in their turn, for once in their lives, to give way to force and endure a humiliation. I am glad for them.[6]

For all her partisanship, it is noteworthy that, while getting in this last word, she recognises that the

material result of the strikes may be disastrous for both
sides. Her strong and passionate feelings seldom obscured her objectivity.

The years 1936–39 were not crammed quite so full
with disasters and suffering as certain other periods of
the twentieth century, but they have undoubtedly
been the most nerve-racking, so far. In Spain, civil war;
in Russia, the Moscow trials and the Stalin terror; in
Germany, the Hitler terror; in France and England, a
numbed stupor and a ferment of communist and
fascist intrigue; and then the capitulation to Hitler at
Munich, and finally the outbreak of war. There must
be very few people who lived through that period
without errors of opinion and behaviour which it now
embarrasses them to recall. In Simone Weil's case,
what she came bitterly to regret later on was her
doctrinaire pacifism of those days. On the whole,
however, her attempt to be realistic and objective
throughout the nightmare was magnificent, even
though not one hundred per cent successful.

By 1934, as we have seen, she had already almost
despaired of the immediate future. The huge, centralised, bureaucratic slave state seemed to her an
inevitable development which humanity is fated to
have to live through until the day when the centralised
mechanism finally jams and the machine explodes.
But she had not quite given up hope and was still
prepared to offer herself to be ground to pieces in the
"endeavour to introduce a little play into the cogs of
the machine which is grinding us down." The purpose,
or at least the chief conscious purpose, of her year in
the Paris factories had been to acquire the necessary
practical experience for performing this role. Immediately after the break with B—— we find her discussing

with Auguste Detoeuf the possibility of working in one of his factories in Paris in order to cooperate with him from the workers' level.[7] Detoeuf was not only a big business man but a big man, and she could talk to him with some hope of being understood. But he probably realised that her health would not stand up to another experience like the one he had procured for her in the Alsthom works.

French politics were dominated in 1936 by the stay-in strikes, the formation of Léon Blum's Popular Front government, and the Spanish Civil War, which broke out at the end of July. Whatever its economic results, the occupation of the factories by the workers had this great value in Simone Weil's eyes: that the workers had for once "lifted their heads," asserted themselves, and made themselves at home, in a place where previously only the machines had been at home and the workers were admitted simply as slaves to tend them. "Is it natural," she wrote afterwards, "that a woman should never be able to see the place where her husband expends the best of himself all day and every day?"[8] (During the strikes she had seen workers proudly showing their families around the workshops.)

But, on the debit side, she clearly recognised the irresponsibility and selfishness of the workers' organisations, which no partisan loyalty could induce her to whitewash. And before long we find her scolding the Popular Front government for its indifference to the oppressed workers in French Africa and Indo-China:

> The Popular Front has been in power for eight months, but no one has yet found time to think about them. When the Billancourt metal-workers have a problem, Léon Blum receives a delegation; he finds time to go to the Exhibition to address the building workers; when he thinks the civil servants are getting glum he gives them a

lovely talk all to themselves on the wireless. But as for the millions of proletarians in the colonies, we have all of us forgotten all about them.[9]

This was written early in 1937, and it must be admitted that there is a somewhat scolding note in a good many of the political articles she wrote at about this time. It suggests that she was writing under strain, which is probable enough in a period when France seemed sometimes to be on the verge of civil war or of a revolution, which might come either from the Right or from the Left. It was a time when, as she put it, private life had become, not only for politicians but for everybody, almost swallowed up by public events. "The permanent conditions of our existence are such as to prevent us from finding in our daily lives any moral resources independent of the political and social situation." And another article of 1937 is a quite effective but rather shrill exercise in sarcasm, which is uncharacteristic of her, and therefore very significant. Sarcasm always indicates strain and repression.

Her pacifist essays, too, are below her best level. They are always well reasoned and sometimes profound, but they too often display a use of logic for buttressing violently extreme opinions which tells the same story as her sarcasm. Her pacifism appears to rest upon two arguments, one of them political and historical and the other psychological and moral. Politically, she opposed the myth of the "revolutionary war." Robespierre was clear-sighted when he tried to prevent France from going to war against the rest of Europe in 1792. That famous war, so far from being a revolutionary war, paved the way for the Napoleonic tyranny. Until the day when the anarchists' ideal of a nonhierarchical army becomes practicable, every war in modern conditions will merely strengthen the centralised bureaucracy against the individual. Therefore

no war can ever advance the cause of freedom.[10] That is
the gist of her political argument.

The moral argument is based upon an important
and extremely just distinction between self-contempt
and humiliation. Is death preferable to dishonour?
Yes, if dishonour means despising oneself, for in that
case to purchase life at the price of dishonour means
"for the sake of life, to lose the reasons for living." But
if dishonour merely means humiliation, then the case
is altered. The slave Epictetus, treated as a puppet by
his master, and Jesus, buffeted and crowned with
thorns, were humiliated; but they were in no way
lowered in their own eyes.

> To prefer death to self-contempt is the foundation of
> every morality; to prefer death to humiliation is some-
> thing quite different, it is simply the feudal point of
> honour.[11]

It is only the individual who can decide whether or not
he despises himself, and if it is by collective and public
force that he is constrained to wipe out some dishonour, then this can have no effect upon his private
self-approval or self-contempt. But in war everyone is
constrained by force. Even volunteers, once they have
enlisted, are forced to accept martial law. And so, with
almost too much logical ingenuity, we reach the
conclusion that "war can never be a means for avoid-
ing self-contempt";[12] from which, with similar ingenuity, it is made to follow that no peace is
disgraceful, whatever the terms of the treaty may be.

These are her ideas of 1936, and presumably she
would have argued in the same way at the time of the
Munich crisis two years later, when, however regret-
fully, she seems to have supported the Chamberlain-
Daladier capitulation. And yet, in the interval, she had
taken part in the Spanish Civil War. The apparent

inconsistency was allowed for in advance, however, in a passage where she says that a man's self-respect can be broken by an outrage suffered by another man or men, "when it is impossible to submit passively to the outrage without accusing oneself of cowardice." [13] However, she renounced her pacifism in 1939, so there is no point in continuing the discussion, except to note that her final position on the subject was characteristically shrewd and fair-minded.

Writing in 1943, she observed that to advocate extreme passive resistance for a whole nation presupposes that nation to be, in the aggregate, sufficiently close to perfection to be able to imitate collectively the passion of Christ. If employed against a sufficiently ruthless invader this method would certainly lead to the nation's disappearance. "But such a disappearance would be worth infinitely more than the most glorious survival." [14] Like most people, however, she believes such perfection on a national scale to be unattainable, but she respects the scruples of those who believe otherwise and who feel called on to bear witness to their belief. She stipulates only that some way should be found for them to be present at the actual scene of war "and present in a much more arduous and more perilous way than is demanded of the soldiers themselves." [15] The point of this stipulation being that it provides the only way of distinguishing between two different kinds of aversion which pacifism often confuses together: the aversion to killing and the aversion to being killed. "The influence of the aversion to killing is not dangerous; in the first place it is a good influence, for it has its origin in goodness; and secondly it is weak and there is unfortunately no chance of its ever becoming otherwise." [16] The fear of being killed, on the other hand, is strong and almost everyone is sometimes possessed by it.

Those who are overcome by it should be treated with compassion; but if they try to turn their weakness into a doctrine to be propagated they become criminal and must be discredited.

Even during her own pacifist phase Simone Weil could be in some ways exceedingly tough-minded. She had not studied Machiavelli for nothing. In 1937, meditating on the fall of Léon Blum's government, she ascribed it to irresolution and weakness:

> If a newly-constituted power, wishing to deal certain blows at its opponents, does so at the beginning and then leaves them more or less in peace, then they will be grateful to it for all the harm they are *not* suffering; if it begins by treating its opponents gently, then later on they will react aggressively to the slightest threat. But worst of all is to be gentle while at the same time alarming them with vague threats which never material-ise; in that way, by incurring hostility and contempt at the same time, one is lost. And that is what has hap-pened.
>
> The fundamental principle of power, and of all politi-cal action, is never to present the appearance of weak-ness. Force not only makes itself feared but it is always also a little bit loved, even by those whom it most violently compels to submit to it. Weakness is not only not feared, but it always inspires a little contempt and repulsion, even in those whom it favours. There is no bitterer truth than this; and this is why it is generally not recognised. . . . The lion crawls to the tamer who appears as an invincible power, and licks his hand; the same lion devours the tamer who has betrayed fear or hesitation. The individual facing the crowd is always a little like the tamer before the lion; and that is the situation of the man in power.[17]

In this and the next three chapters I am concerned less with Simone Weil's ideas than with her life and character. I shall try farther on to give an outline of her thought, and it will then be seen that the stark realism of the passage just quoted is a most essential part of her outlook. But in describing her character it is even more essential to bring out the altogether extraordinary passion for justice, the sympathy, and the love for individuals. The passion for justice is conspicuous in all her writing, combined with an unflinching recognition of its almost total absence in human behaviour, as everywhere else; but her interest in individual human beings sometimes has to be read between the lines. She seldom attempted descriptive psychology. Nevertheless, there is one very valuable and rather unexpected source of information about her contacts with people, namely, the diary she kept of her year as a factory worker. A great part of it consists of technical notes, calculations of pay rates, sketches of machine parts, and descriptions of factory organisation. But there are also a certain number of human oases. She describes, for example, how she was working at a furnace in the Alsthom factory, having to raise and lower the shutter, which meant repeatedly getting her arms scorched; but there was a welder working near by who smiled at her with sympathy each time it happened, which made an incalculable difference.

And here is an almost idyllic sketch of two unemployed fitters whom she met while looking for a new job after leaving Alsthom. One of them was underfed, and although she doesn't say so, she herself was almost certainly in the same condition, as she was living on her pay and was between jobs. It is interesting that in this passage—as always in her diary and in her letters of the factory period—she uses figures instead of words for numerals.

Wednesday—(divine weather) with 2 fitters. One aged 18. The other 58. *Very* interesting, but extremely reserved. But obviously a real man. Living alone (wife left him). His big interest is his hobby, photography. "They killed the cinema with the Talkies, instead of letting it be what it really is, the most perfect development of photography." . . . Affects a certain cynicism. But obviously a man of heart.

Conversation between the 3 of us the whole morning, extraordinarily free, easy, on a level above the petty miseries of life which are the overriding preoccupation of slaves, especially women. What a relief, after Alsthom!

The young one is interesting too. As we were going along by Saint-Cloud he said: "If I were in form (he isn't, alas, because he's hungry) I should draw—Everyone has something that interests him." "For me, says the other one, it's photography." The young one asks me: "And you, what is your passion?" Embarrassed, I answer: "Reading." And he: "Yes, I can imagine that. But not novels. More philosophic, wouldn't it be?" Then we talk about Zola, and Jack London.

Clearly, both of them have revolutionary tendencies (but that's quite the wrong word—no, say rather that they have class awareness and the spirit of free men.) But when we get on to national defence we no longer agree. However, I don't insist.

Complete comradeship. For the first time in my life, really. No barrier, either in class difference (because it has been eliminated), or in sex. Miraculous.[18]

One feels glad that she spared them a lecture on pacifism.

And finally, by way of contrast, here is a laconic sketch of a woman worker who was an intellectual disappointment:

> . . . has a Schwärmerei for Tolstoy (*Resurrection:* "sublime", "that man understood love").[19]

And since there are so few records of her undoubtedly very frequent sympathetic human contacts, here is one more, from a later period, when she was in Milan on holiday:

> The people are really sympathetic. I am writing this at a delightful little café in Piazza Beccaria; just now the waiter was peeping over my shoulder at what I was writing, and when I looked up his smile was charming.[20]

To resume the biographical thread—when Simone Weil's collaboration with B—— broke down, the summer vacation was beginning, and she left Bourges for Paris, where she managed to get into the Renault works during the stay-in strike and see her former workmates in possession. She also held earnest discussions with Detoeuf, suggesting to him that on the resumption of work the employers should say to the victorious strikers: "You decided to demonstrate your strength. Very good. But this has created a situation without precedent, which calls for new forms of organisation. Since you intend to compel industrial enterprises to acknowledge the force of your claims, you must be able to face the responsibilities of the new situation you have brought about." [21] After which they should make every effort to keep the workers, or at least their delegates, fully informed of all the technical and organisational and commercial problems of the business. This sounds utopian, but in one of Detoeuf's own factories and with Simone Weil as one of the delegates, who knows if it might not have worked?

During that summer vacation, however, the Spanish Civil War broke out, and early in August, when the war was only a few weeks old, she took the train to Barcelona. Within a few days of arriving she was on the Aragon front with the Durruti column of the Anarchist forces. Out of loyalty to her pacifist principles she had made an effort not to feel morally involved in the war but, as she wrote two years later to Bernanos, she had found it impossible to stop wishing all day and every day for the victory of one side; and there was, as we have seen, a loophole in her pacifism —namely, the case of an outrage against other people "to which it is impossible to submit passively without accusing oneself of cowardice." It was through this loophole that she escaped from Paris to Spain.

The few pages of her Spanish journal give tantalising glimpses of the early days of the war and it is a great loss that, apart from the long letter to Bernanos, she wrote no more about it. The journal also shows how fortunate it is that during her brief stay in Spain the tolerant anarchist ethic was still in the ascendant. It is obvious that she was not prepared to sacrifice an atom of her independence of mind and judgement, and this attitude, displayed as she would have displayed it, was to become within a matter of weeks rather than months almost suicidally dangerous. In the first few days she was enthusiastic, though without losing her head:

> This is one of those extraordinary periods, which hitherto have never lasted long, when those who have always been subordinate assume responsibility. This involves a few disadvantages, to be sure. When one gives loaded rifles to lads of seventeen in the midst of an unarmed populace ... [22]

She interrogates peasants in the village of Pina and notes that all of them consider life in towns to be much better than in the country; and that they have a marked sense of inferiority to the Anarchist soldiers from Barcelona. (She told Bernanos that the soldiers in their turn were offhand and condescending, and that the gulf between peasants and soldiers was exactly

like the gulf between poor and rich.) Soon she is given
a rifle and finds herself attached to a multiracial group
of skirmishers—French, Catalan and German. There is
no continuous front line but there is a kind of no
man's land along the river Ebro. A "vague" bombardment occurs and a very small bomb is dropped. "Felt
no emotion at all." She takes part in a fatigue to cross
the river and burn some enemy corpses. There is some
talk about a raid, which appears to end in a decision to
postpone it until the morrow. Then, suddenly, she
realises that the raid, on a house a short distance away,
is actually taking place and that she is in it. "At that
moment, *great* emotion (I don't know what the point
of the raid is, and I do know that if one is captured one
is shot.)" On a later page she notes that if she is made
prisoner and shot it will only be justice, because she is
the moral accomplice of similar atrocities on her own
side. This particular raid, however, ends without incident. They wait in a ditch while five of the party crawl
up to the house. They hear sounds of talking, and then
the five reappear, and they all return across the river.
"This was the first and *only* time I felt frightened
during my stay at Pina."

All the same, a day and a half later, at 2:30 A.M., she
is setting off as a volunteer on another similar expedition and "only half pleased" about it. This time
reconnaissance planes come over and there is a heavy
bombardment, but once again no hand-to-hand fight-
ing. They return with a family of peasants who have
been removed, presumably for their own safety, from
the house in no man's land. She notes that they
respond half-heartedly to the clenched fist salute and
thinks it cruel to make them do it, since they are obviously not sympathisers.

The diary ends with some notes on collectivised
factories and a brief reference to the ten revenge

murders in Sitges after the failure of the Majorca expedition. She was in hospital at Sitges at the time, but she says nothing about the fortunate accident with cooking oil which brought her there and led to her departure for France. It certainly saved her life. With her inability to refrain from volunteering for any danger and her equal inability to refrain from protesting at any physical or moral injustice, she could not have lasted long in the Spanish Civil War. By the time she wrote her letter to Bernanos, in 1938, she had already seen it confirm, or at least appear to support, her theory that no war can ever advance the cause of freedom but only strengthen bureaucracy against the individual. The Spanish war had become a battle of wits between the Russian and German bureaucracies, using the starved and massacred Spanish people as pawns.

ON HER RETURN from Spain in September, 1936, Simone Weil's father persuaded her to obtain a year's leave from teaching, and by the following Spring her burns were sufficiently healed for her to take a strenuous holiday in Italy. She stopped in Milan, Florence, Rome, and Assisi, and wrote an exuberant series of letters about it to her friend Jean Posternak, then a young medical student undergoing a cure at Montana.[1] "Don't forget," she wrote to him, "if you are sending me any useful tips, to deal not only with works of art but also with interesting quarters of towns, and restaurants, and any spectacles of low life or high life, so long as they are characteristic ... As you know, everything interests me." In another letter she told him that Italy had reawakened her impulse to write poetry, which she had repressed "for various reasons" since adolescence. This is certainly significant, and what it signifies, I think, is that it was during this journey that the second and more mysterious phase of her life began.

Not that it is possible to divide her life into two distinct phases, or even to indicate any clear-cut change either in her essential beliefs or in her behaviour. But there was a change in her language which indicates some new development in her outlook. For example, in 1942 she would write to Joë Bousquet, a friend who was incurably paralysed from a wound in the First World War:

> I am going to say something which is painful to think, more painful to say, and almost unbearably painful to say to those one loves. For anyone in affliction, evil can perhaps be defined as being everything that gives any consolation.[2]

This is a fairly startling pronouncement, but it is only a development from the belief she held at the age of fourteen, that if we desire bread we do not receive stones; bread meaning the truth and everything good. Affliction, she had come to believe, is a supreme school of truth; and therefore to seek to ease it with consolations, which are never true but always illusory, is to accept stones in place of bread. These ideas will require further elucidation, but it can be seen that they are consistent with her previous outlook. In the same letter to Joë Bousquet, however, she says:

> I would never dare to speak to you like this if all these thoughts were the product of my own mind. But although I am unwilling to place any reliance on such impressions, I do really have the feeling, in spite of myself, that God is addressing all this to you, for love of you, through me.[3]

This is a new note, and some readers may find it a disconcerting one. But that is an unreasonable reaction unless one has first ascertained what the idea of God speaking through a human being may have meant to Simone Weil; and this idea, like her idea of the spirituality of labour, is one which any book about her must aim to elucidate. A perfect elucidation of either of these ideas would be equivalent to a perfect exposition of her thought; but it is not possible even to approach the task without first completing the pre-

liminary sketch of her life. She wrote to Bernanos in
1938 that "nothing that is Catholic, nothing that is
Christian, has ever seemed alien" to her, and in the
letter to Father Perrin, from which I have already
quoted, she says in effect that she has always been
aware of possessing a naturally Christian soul, adding,
however, that she has never at any time "sought for
God" and that the very expression "search for God"
seems to her a false one. It appeared to her while she
was still adolescent, she continues, that the data for
solving the problem of God are not obtainable in this
world and that it was therefore useless to attempt to
solve it.

> For I thought that being in this world, our business was
> to adopt the best attitude with regard to the problems of
> this world and that such an attitude did not depend
> upon the solution of the problem of God.[4]

For a long time, therefore, as she puts it, "the very
name of God had no place in her thoughts," and
certainly during the whole period that we have been
studying, up to the end of her stay in Spain, there is
little or nothing in her writing to suggest that the word
God was in her thoughts. She was, however, a profound student of Plato, and the epigraphs of her more
important political essays of 1933 and 1934 are taken
from Sophocles, Marcus Aurelius, and Spinoza; and it
is difficult to think of any of those four deeply religious
thinkers without thinking of some conception of God.
But it remains true that whatever she may have
thought about the various conceptions of God, it was
love and justice between men, conceived exclusively as
a problem of human life in this world, that was the
only conscious motive of all her activity.

Sometime between 1935 and 1940 her outlook
broadened and deepened; but this was a new develop-

ment and not a change of mind. It would be an understatement to say that nothing was changed except her manner of expressing herself and that what she had to express was exactly the same. But it would be completely untrue to say that what she had to express was something different. What happened was that she found more of it to express and that she required a new vocabulary for doing so. The first symptom of this new development appears as early as 1935, after she left the Renault factory, when her parents took her for a holiday to Portugal before she resumed teaching. She describes in her letter to Father Perrin how her year of factory work had made her fully aware for the first time of something that she had always known in theory but only partially experienced: the reality of affliction, as experienced by the "anonymous mass" of humanity. The sense of servitude was burnt into her so deeply that "still today [seven years later] whenever any human being, whoever it is and in whatever circumstances, speaks to me without brutality, I cannot help having the impression that there must be a mistake." [5]

This reaction may appear at first sight morbidly excessive. There were, after all, as her journal and her letters of the time bear witness, some oases of kindness and comradeship in her factory life. But Simone Weil lived on two levels simultaneously. On the personal level, she could have adapted herself to an even harder life; but on the impersonal level she was capable, in a way that most people are not, of suffering from a system which outraged her principles, irrespective of whether her personal experience of it was pleasant or unpleasant.

In any case, and for whatever reason, she was in a state of extreme physical and mental exhaustion during the Portuguese holiday; and it so happened that

she found herself alone one evening, under a full
moon, in a very poor fishing village. By chance it was
the day of its patron saint, and the women were
visiting all the ships in procession, with candles, and
chanting "what must certainly be very ancient hymns
of a heart-rending sadness."

> There, the certainty suddenly came to me that Chris-
> tianity is pre-eminently the religion of slaves, that slaves
> cannot help adhering to it, and I among the others.[6]

I do not remember any other reference to this experience in her work; but, as already noted, her public
behaviour after it, in Bourges, Paris, and Spain, was
anything but servile.

Her description of her feelings in the Portuguese
village raises the question of what she meant by
"adhering" to a religion. She was later to write about
Catholicism in a way that could give rise to various
interpretations; but her own clearest interpretation of
the word "adherence" is the one she gave in a passage
of her notebooks, written about six years later. She
calls it an adherence of the mind, or spirit (*adhésion
d'esprit*), analogous to what one gives to a work of art.
The complete passage is as follows:

> Belief. Very different meanings. $2 + 2 = 4$, or: I am
> holding this pen. Here, belief is the feeling of evidence.
> I cannot, by definition, believe in mysteries in this way.
> But I believe that the mysteries of the Catholic religion
> are an inexhaustible source of truths concerning the
> human condition. (And further, they are for me an ob-
> ject of love.) Only nothing prevents me from believing
> that some of those truths have been directly revealed
> elsewhere. Adherence of the mind analogous to what is
> obtained by a work of art (the very greatest art).[7]

In this sense, as we shall see, she adhered to more than
one religion.

After the experience in Portugal, the next incident symptomatic of a change in her outlook occurred during the holiday in Italy in 1937. Having spent Whitsun in Rome, she went on to Assisi, and her letters to Jean Posternak tell a great deal about her impressions but they say nothing about this particular incident. Once again, as with the Portuguese incident, I cannot remember that she ever referred to it except in her letter to Father Perrin. What happened was that when she was alone in the twelfth century chapel of Santa Maria degli Angeli, where Saint Francis himself often prayed, she found herself for the first time in her life kneeling down as if to pray—impelled "by something stronger than myself."

To kneel in the chapel of Saint Francis was poetically appropriate to her feelings; but it was not an intentional act of prayer. Years afterwards she was still distrustful of the power of suggestion that goes with prayer, "the power for which Pascal recommends it. Pascal's method seems to me one of the worst possible for arriving at faith." [8]

On her return to Paris from Italy her spirits seem to have suffered a bad relapse from the buoyancy which she displayed throughout the Italian holiday. She recommenced teaching, at the Lycée of St. Quentin, in October, 1937, but had to stop after four months because of violent and chronic headaches. Nevertheless, the essays and articles she wrote in 1937 are vigorous and pungent, though the scolding note, to which I have already referred, was sometimes in evidence. She gave a lecture on taylorisation (rationalisation) to a working class audience, in which she of course attacked it, while pointing out at the same time that an attack on rationalisation was distinct from an attack on the property system. The workers can win rights for themselves in a factory without dispossessing the owners, while they can find themselves completely without rights in a collectivised and rationalised factory. She also warned her audience against the scientific prestige of rationalisation. Scientists can be bought, and a totalitarian government can even impose its own "scientific" truths. (This was just after some German scientists had obediently discovered that the human organism requires less fat in its diet than had previously been believed.)

But her most important essay in 1937 was "The Power of Words" (*Ne recommençons pas la guerre de Troie*).[9] This is a brilliantly clear-headed and lucid plea for the discrediting of jargon, as a first step towards realistic political thinking; and one would never guess that the author was racked by headaches or that her sense of participation in human affliction, not only in the present but in all ages, had reduced her to feeling like a slave. One might, however, perhaps read into it that she is beginning to feel disillusioned about the possibility of effective political action, although she no doubt hoped that the essay would persuade its readers that war might still be avoided.

In 1938, to judge by her published work, she wrote comparatively little. But she published a note on the French colonial problem in which she suggested that one other good result—in addition to the (vainly) hoped-for avoidance of war—might emerge from the Munich agreement of that year. France's loss of prestige in Europe had made her Empire all the more necessary to her for maintaining her position in the world, but she was too weak to keep her Empire together unless she could persuade the colonial peoples to *want* to remain in it. Thus Munich might indirectly benefit the French colonial peoples.

When she discussed the colonial problem again, in 1943, France was even weaker, but Simone Weil still hoped that after the war a better understanding between the French and the colonial peoples might be reached. By this time, however, she was much more critical of the effects of westernisation upon oriental peoples, and she considered it was the West which required a dose of orientalism rather than vice versa. She correctly foresaw, too, that what we are in fact likely to get from the East is the opposite of anything that could be called oriental influence; it is a double dose of our own western medicine. About Africa, on the other hand, her views of 1943 read strangely today in the light of what has since happened. There are all too many Nation-States in the world already, she thought, and it would be disastrous to create a lot of new ones in Africa.

From 1939 onwards she makes the impression, in her writing, of a runner who has found his second wind. Beginning with her great essays, "The 'Iliad,' Poem of Force," [10] and "The Great Beast" (*Quelques réflexions sur les origines de l'Hitlérisme*), [11] she goes on from strength to strength. The latter essay, in which she compares modern totalitarianism with the system of ancient Rome, reveals her wide and profound knowledge of European and classical history—though it also reveals what one might almost call a totalitarian hatred of Rome, which is too extreme to be realistic. In the following year she wrote some of the essays which appeared after her death in *Pensées sans ordre concernant l'amour de Dieu*; she commenced the series of notebooks which are among the most important intellectual documents of our time and which can be, and have been, compared to the *Pensées* of Pascal; and she began to write a drama, mostly in verse, on the theme of the Spanish conspiracy at Venice in 1618 (the same theme as Otway's *Venice Preserved*). She continued to work at intervals upon this drama until the end of her life.[12]

At approximately the same time, that is to say in 1938–39, her personal life also entered into a new phase, related to the experiences in Portugal and Assisi.

I referred in the first chapter to T. S. Eliot's comparison of Simone Weil's genius to that of the saints, and I undertook to describe that genius from the point of view that symptoms of abnormality should be assumed to arise from some defect, in the sense of maladjustment, unless they can be demonstrated to arise from a finer than average adjustment to life—by which I mean a superiority in intelligence, courage, sensitiveness, and love. Up to 1938, when her headaches appear to have reached a crisis of intensity, it seems to me obvious that, in spite of a certain violence of feeling and a headstrong singlemindedness which led to occasional errors of judgement, she showed much more intelligence, maturity, and sophistication, more detachment in her political and psychological appreciations, and far more courage, unselfishness, and determination in her behaviour, than one would normally expect from a comfortably nurtured and socially privileged Parisian intellectual in her twenties. And apart from these obvious superiorities one could maintain that there was nothing particularly mysterious about her. But during the last three or four years of her life it becomes impossible to ignore what looks like an unbalanced tendency towards self-immolation, an intensity of self-sacrifice, which cannot be regarded as simply a high degree of any common virtues, such as unselfishness or courage. Whatever else it is, it is certainly abnormal.

Without attempting to prejudge it, one must recognise that her personal life, as described by Catholic friends whom she got to know in Marseilles in 1941 and as revealed by some of her letters from New York and London in 1942 and 1943, seems to have been lived most of the time during those years in that abnormal state. But, concurrently, her writing became more and more cogent, lucid and profound, culminating, in 1943, in several incomparable essays and one book, *The Need for Roots*, which perhaps contains more of what the present age most needs to be made to understand and more of the criticism to which it most needs to be made to listen than any other writer of this century has been able to express.

Her mystical experiences, and what she wrote about them, must be given due weight in any account of her life. But it cannot be too strongly emphasised that her ethical and metaphysical and psychological and historical ideas exist in their own right and could be studied with the same effect if all trace of the woman who expressed them, and her abnormal experiences and her abnormal behaviour, had disappeared. And this is in fact precisely how, according to her own theory, they ought to be studied.

Nevertheless, we are entitled to study what she herself wrote about her mystical experiences. At Easter, 1938, after she had been compelled by her headaches to stop teaching and while the headaches were still in their acutest phase, she went with her mother to Solesmes to hear the Gregorian music at the Easter services. Inspired, so far as she was aware, by no more than an aesthetic impulse, she succeeded in attending to the music in spite of her pain.

> An extreme effort of attention enabled me to get outside this miserable flesh, leaving it to suffer by itself, heaped up in its corner, and to find a pure and perfect joy in the unspeakable beauty of the chanting and the words. This

experience enabled me by analogy to understand better the possibility of loving the divine love in the midst of affliction.[13]

During the ten days she spent at Solesmes she made the acquaintance of an undergraduate from Oxford who, she says, was a true angel, or messenger, because he introduced her to the seventeenth-century English metaphysical poets. Settling down to read them with her usual thoroughness, she picked especially upon George Herbert's "Love," and from then on when her headache was at a particularly painful crisis she would recite the poem to herself, "fixing all my attention on it and clinging with all my soul to the tenderness it enshrines." As with the Gregorian music, she supposed her attachment to the poem to be aesthetic and believed that she was reciting it simply as a beautiful poem.

Love bade me welcome: yet my soul drew back,
Guiltie of dust and sinne.

. . . .

"You must sit down, "sayes Love, "and taste my meat":
So I did sit and eat.

But, as she puts it, the recitation had, without her knowing it, the virtue of a prayer and one day while she was reciting the poem "Christ himself came down and took possession of me." That is how she described the experience to Father Perrin four years later, in 1942, and unless I am mistaken the only other occasion on which she wrote about it [14] was in her letter to Joë Bousquet of May 12 in the same year, when she said this:

At a moment of intense physical pain, when I was making the effort to love, although believing I had no right to give any name to the love, I felt, while completely unprepared for it (I had never read the mystics), a presence more personal, more certain, and more real than that of any human being; it was inaccessible both to sense and to imagination, and it resembled the love that irradiates the tenderest smile of somebody one loves.[15]

(One is reminded of the furnace which scorched her arms in the factory, and the welder who smiled at her with sympathy.) Since she says this happened "about three and a half years ago," it must have been at the end of 1938. It was in 1939 that she began to write her essay on the *Iliad* and on the origins of Hitlerism, which appear to me to mark the beginning of a renaissance in her writing.

To Father Perrin, as to Joë Bousquet, she emphasises that "neither my senses nor my imagination had any part" in the experience. She, therefore, had no hallucination of the senses. She saw, heard, and touched nothing, but simply felt in the midst of acute pain the presence of a love like that which one can read in the smile on a beloved face. And she associated this love with Christ.

Every reader will interpret this experience as best he can. She certainly regarded it as the supreme experience of her life, and her own explanation of it, which we shall find to be easily deducible from some of her later writings, seems to me the simplest and clearest. It derives from her conception of what she called "the other reality." But there is also a note, written in 1942, in *La Connaissance surnaturelle*, which suggests that she sometimes inclined to an explanation very similar to what any conventional rationalist might give; though its interpretation would be beyond him. This is the note:

> If love finds no object, the lover must love his love itself, perceived as something external. Then one has found God.
> "*Amare amabam*." If he had stuck to that, he had found the way.[16]

(When she speaks of love finding "no object," she means of course no ultimately satisfying object). From this point of view, the presence she was aware of, "more personal, more certain, and more real than that of any human being," would be that of her own love, exteriorised. I shall try to show, however, that the various explanations are no more than verbally incompatible, and that it is necessary to understand this before one can begin to understand Simone Weil.

One of the first results of the experience was to make her discover Christian values in other and older religious and philosophical traditions—in Plato, in the Bhagavad-Gita, in the Tao, in the religions of Dionysus and Osiris. About three years later, however, the possibility of her being baptised into the Catholic Church was suggested to her, and she seems to imply that it might indeed have been possible for her if the Church were as catholic in fact as it ought to be by right. But she reproaches it with a sort of provincialism both in space and time:

> There are so many things outside it; so many things that I love and do not want to relinquish, so many things that God loves, or else they would not exist. The whole immense vista of past centuries, except for the last twenty; all the countries inhabited by the colored races; all secular life in the white people's countries; and in the history of those countries all the traditions banned as heretical—the Manichaean and Albigensian, for example; and all the things that came out of the Renaissance, too often degraded, but not altogether without value.[17]

She was not baptised, and there is much in her letters to Father Perrin, from which the above is quoted, which makes it seem strange that she was even able to consider it as a possibility. It becomes even stranger in the light of what she wrote in her last letter to him:

The Church is in fact for you, as well as being your link with the heavenly fatherland, also an earthly fatherland. You live there in an atmosphere of human warmth. That makes a little attachment almost inevitable.

Such an attachment is perhaps for you that infinitely fine thread of which St. John of the Cross speaks, which, so long as it is not broken, holds the bird down to the ground as effectively as a thick metal chain; I imagine that the last thread, although very fine, must be the hardest to cut, because when it is cut one has to fly, and that is frightening. But all the same the obligation is imperative.

The children of God ought not to have any other fatherland here below except the universe itself, with the totality of all the reasoning creatures it ever has contained, contains, or ever will contain. That is the native city to which we owe our love.[18]

Nevertheless, it remains true that her own attitude towards the Church, although she frequently writes as its uncompromising intellectual critic, continued to be complex, not to say obscure. The reason may perhaps be that she did not always make it clear—perhaps not even to herself—whether she was thinking of Catholicism as she believed it ought to be by right, or as she considered it to be in fact.

6 "OUR DAILY BREAD"

CRITICS OF SIMONE WEIL who are upset by her apparent change of orientation after 1938 sometimes suggest that her mysticism was an example of the well-known phenomenon of the disappointed revolutionary who subsides into a comfortable other-worldly quietism. But in her case the conviction of contact with a real and certain extra-terrestrial love made her if possible more passionately concerned than ever about the problem of affliction in the world. In the early days of the war, before the collapse of France in June, 1940, she worked out a scheme for employing women in the most dangerous parts of the front line to give summary first aid in cases of shock, burns, and loss of blood. She presented it frankly as a kind of suicide corps but pointed out, with considerable show of reason, that from the propaganda point of view it would be the perfect answer to Hitler's special groups of young men, S. S. and parachutists, who were not merely prepared to risk their lives but to face certain death.

If one may believe neutral reports, they exhibit at the front the heroism of brutality, and carry it to the extreme possible limits of courage. To demonstrate to the world that we are worth more than our enemies, we cannot claim to have more courage, because that would be quantitatively impossible. But we can and ought to demonstrate that our courage is qualitatively different, is courage of a more difficult and rarer kind. . . . There could be no better symbol of our inspiration than the corps of women suggested here. The mere persistence of a few human services in the very centre of the battle, the climax of inhumanity, would be a signal defiance of the inhumanity which the enemy has chosen for himself and which he compels us also to practise. . . . Although composed of unarmed women, it would certainly impress the enemy soldiers, in the sense that their presence and their behaviour would be a new and unexpected revelation of the depth of the moral resources and resolution on our side.[1]

This scheme was apparently not turned down at sight by the army, as the product of romantic-patriotic hysteria. Exactly how it was received is obscure, but Simone Weil believed that if the front had not collapsed in June, 1940, it would have had some chance of being tried out on a small scale. It had the merit of extreme simplicity, and she was able to demonstrate from army medical publications that an elementary equipment for plasma injections could in fact enable an almost untrained woman to save lives in cases of shock, burns, and hemorrhage by applying first aid in the field, immediately after the shock or wound had been received.

Nevertheless, one does sense behind this scheme an almost feverishly self-immolating spirit, and it is a striking example of human complexity that at the very time when she was trying to procure a suicidal mission for herself she was engaged in a long correspondence with her brother about the effects of the discovery of incommensurables in the fifth century B.C.

There may well have been crisis and scandal among minds of inferior scientific and philosophic formation. It is indeed more than likely. Who knows if the demonstration of the even being equal to the odd may not have been the model for the demonstrations proving a thesis and its contrary (the basis of sophistry) which pullulated in the fifth century and demoralised Athens? [2]

It is equally striking that she was at work at the same time on her essays "The 'Iliad,' Poem of Force" and "The Great Beast." In the last four marvellous pages of the *Iliad* essay she introduces most of the themes of her later work, and one is tempted to wish that she could have developed them in serene and scholarly seclusion. But life is not like that. The Olympian Goethe is an exception, and it is much more usual for real and original thought to be won from a hard and bitter life.

> *Out of a stem that scored the hand*
> *I wrung it in a weary land.*

It is bitterness that Simone Weil finds in the *Iliad*, and she calls it the *only* justifiable bitterness; because it springs from the subjection of the human spirit to force, which means, in the last analysis, to matter. One may paraphrase her argument as follows: The *Iliad* is the one great epic poem of the West. (Note that she limits this judgement to western literature.) Its greatness consists in its true portrayal of the subjection of all men, without exception, to the domination of material forces. The Greeks, in general, possessed that rare power of soul which enables men to avoid self-deception; and what makes the *Iliad* miraculous is that its bitterness is directed solely against the tragedy of the subjection of the human spirit.

> This subjection is the common human lot, although each spirit will bear it differently, in proportion to its own virtue. No one in the *Iliad* is spared by it, as no one on earth is. No one who succumbs to it is by virtue of this fact regarded with contempt. Whoever, within his

own soul and in human relations, escapes the dominion
of force is loved but loved sorrowfully because of the
threat of destruction that constantly hangs over him.[3]

Simone Weil has written so much about the oppression of men by men that a superficial reader of her
political and historical essays might imagine that the
dominion of force meant for her the coercion of the
many by the selfish power of the few, or of enlightened
minorities by the crowd, which, following Plato, she
called "the social beast." But these are only two
particular illustrations of her general point. What she
is essentially concerned with is the universal enslavement of the human spirit—to passion, to inertia, to
material necessity, to herd-values, and above all to
self-deception. It is for their courageous recognition of
this fact that she admires the Greeks; and she finds the
Greek spirit expressed in its perfection only in the
Iliad, in a few Greek tragedies, and in the Gospels.
Even in the style of the Gospels she finds phrases
which recall Homer, as when Christ says to Peter:
"Another shall gird thee and carry thee whither thou
wouldst not." We shall return later to her belief in the
unity of the Greek spirit with the Christian, and will
only note here that the *Iliad* essay contains a typical
expression of her hostility to the Romans and Hebrews. In the Old Testament she finds very little, apart
from the Book of Job, that is comparable to the Greek
epic; and as for the Romans: "In Rome gladiatorial
fights took the place of tragedy." Her explanation is
the following:

Both the Romans and the Hebrews believed themselves
exempt from the misery that is the common human lot.
The Romans saw themselves as the nation chosen to be
mistress of the world; with the Hebrews it was their God
who exalted them and they retained their superior

position just as long as they obeyed Him. Strangers, enemies, conquered peoples, subjects, slaves, were objects of contempt to the Romans. . . . With the Hebrews, misfortune was a sure indication of sin and hence a legitimate object of contempt; for them a vanquished enemy was abhorrent to God himself.[4]

Whereas in the *Iliad* pity for the fallen is so impartial that one would hardly guess that the writer was Greek and not Trojan.

Since the Gospels were written, she concludes, there has been no revival of the Greek genius. There have been flashes from time to time, in Shakespeare and others, but nothing the peoples of Europe have produced is worth the first known poem that appeared among them.

Perhaps they will yet rediscover the epic genius, when they learn to believe that nothing is immune from blind fatality, when they learn never to admire force and not to hate enemies and not to despise the unfortunate. How soon this will happen is another question.[5]

In the essay on the origins of Hitlerism the Roman Empire is presented as a totalitarian bureaucracy differing from all previous empires, except possibly the Assyrian, in that it had no effective religion except the reason of State. This is a long essay of more than fifty pages, divided into three parts. It traces the influence upon European history of the Roman example of grandeur. Admiration for Rome, says Simone Weil, has practically negated in Europe the influence of the Greek and Christian spirit. It was the Roman example which inspired, consciously or unconsciously, all the great architects of the modern Nation-State—Richelieu, Frederick II, and Napoleon. And Hitler in particular is the most remarkable imitator of Rome who has yet appeared.

The only part of this essay which the French censor

allowed to appear in 1940 was the second part, which describes Rome's diplomacy and methods of conquest and compares them with Hitler's. France being at war with Germany and Italy, criticism of Hitler and Rome was in order; but criticism of Richelieu, Louis XIV, and Napoleon was tabu.

The *Iliad* essay was written for the *Nouvelle Revue Française*, but after the occupation of Paris by the Germans it could not appear there. Simone Weil, having failed to find a way of escaping to England to join the Free French, accompanied her parents to Marseilles, and the essay was published there in the *Cahiers du Sud*.

In Marseilles she made friends with Father J.-M. Perrin, who was then at the Dominican Convent, and there ensued the remarkable correspondence with him, to which we have already referred, about the question of her baptism. The tone of all her letters to Father Perrin is similar to that of the letter to Joë Bousquet, previously quoted, and the same tone of religious intensity is found in her great essay, "The love of God and affliction," and in some other pieces written in 1941 and 1942. On the other hand her notebooks, to which she must have devoted a lot of work at this time, and her writings of 1943 are mostly in her habitual style, which has more of the intellectual calm that one would expect in a pupil of Alain and of the Ecole Normale.

Characteristically, having failed to get to England to join the Free French, she soon formed the project of experiencing on the land a similar ordeal to the one she had previously experienced in factories; but there seems to be this difference, that her personal experience of industrial labour had the practical advantage of helping her to understand the major political and social problem of the moment. (As she wrote in a letter of 1935, how many of the Bolshevik leaders had ever worked in a factory? And if they hadn't, how could they know anything about the real conditions which make servitude or freedom for the workers?) [6] It could be said, of course, that the same applies to work on the land, but in 1941 there was no immediate prospect of turning the experience to account, as she did with the factory experience, and one feels that it had rather a sort of symbolic significance for her. She wanted, before she died, to have experienced all the forms of human bondage to dire necessity. She always hoped to have the experience of prison, and in New York in 1942 she became so obsessed with the negro problem and spent so much time in Harlem that a friend said of her that "if Simone had stayed in America she would surely have become a Negress."

In Marseilles she consulted Father Perrin about getting an agricultural job, and he had the very happy idea of sending her to Gustave Thibon, in the Ardèche, about half way between Lyons and the Mediterranean, on the right bank of the Rhône. M. Thibon arranged for her to work in the grape harvest of a neighbouring farmer. The two descriptions M. Thibon wrote of her are models of personal reminicence. [7] He combines perspicacity with affectionate humour (an ingredient too often lacking in talk about Simone Weil) and with a profound humility before the extraordinary qualities he discerned in the strange and disconcerting young person who had invaded his life. She made him laugh by her awkwardness at the sink, she shocked him by calling Victor Hugo a "*sonore imbécile*," she irritated him by inconveniencing his household through her determination to make herself uncomfortable. This attitude, he thought, amounted to a lack of consideration for others. As he wittily and shrewdly puts it: "In the great volume of the universe, as she read it, her ego was like a word which she had succeeded, perhaps, in *erasing*, but it was still *underlined*." There emanated from her, he says, an aura of strangeness and affliction; but of her genius, both moral and intellectual, he had no doubt, and he attributed the socially awkward side of her character to immaturity. The rarest fruits are often the hardest before they ripen. She read Greek with him and astounded him with her expository gifts, which she lavished with equal generosity on any backward village boy who needed help with his arithmetic. Sometimes, however, according to M. Thibon, she made grotesque psychological errors; attributing a gift for abstract thought to people entirely lacking it and mystifying them by her attempts to interest them in ideas which they found meaningless.

It was while working in the grape harvest in the autumn of 1941 that she began, for the first time in her life, to pray, repeating to herself the Greek text of the Lord's Prayer as she drove herself to keep up with the sturdy peasants working alongside her. She later said that one of her visions of hell was eternal work in a vineyard; but she persevered to the end, and it was on this occasion that the farmer paid her the compliment that she would make a fit wife for a peasant.

It must have have been soon after this that she wrote her commentary on the Lord's Prayer. An adequate comment on this commentary would more than fill this book, and I can only refer here to her translation of the petition "Give us this day our daily bread." It is characteristic that she follows Jerome in translating τὸν ἄρτον ἡμῶν τὸν ἐπιούσιον as "our supernatural bread." As we have seen, she already knew at the age of fourteen that spiritual goods are the only ones

that come in response to our desire, and to pray for
material bread would have seemed to her an abuse.
She points out, however, that it is not only bread in
the literal sense that is necessary to us but also all the
other stimulants which are a source of energy. We
draw energy from outside us and use it up continually,
and if the sources of energy fail we die. Stimulants like
money, ambition, consideration, decorations, power,
celebrity, affection—everything that stimulates our
capacity for action is like bread; and if we are deprived
of some stimulant upon which we have come to de-
pend, it can kill us as surely as hunger.

> All these objects of attachment, as well as food in the
> ordinary sense of the word, make up the daily bread of
> this world. It depends entirely on circumstances whether
> we get it or not. We ought not to ask anything of
> circumstances except that they should conform to the
> will of God. We ought not to ask for the bread of this
> world.[8]

What she meant by supernatural bread, we shall see
later.

Simone Weil was intellectually more mature at fourteen than many people ever become; but at the age of
thirty-two M. Thibon judged her in some ways imma-
ture. Not being a shallow post-Freudian psychologist,
he did not mean that she was "repressed"; he meant
that thirty-two years had not been enough for her to
learn to live with her genius. But there are critics who
would resort to some threadbare commonplace like
sex-repression to account for the self-immolating tendency which dominated her from 1940 onwards, if not
all her life; and this is perhaps the place to meet them.
In writing about any one aspect of anybody one is
bound to falsify, because people are not subdivisible;

and this is particularly true of Simone Weil, who was not an academic theorist but a woman who lived her ideas and whose ideas are in any case too original to be classified—as I have more than once been guilty in these pages of trying to do—under such headings as ethics, psychology, philosophy, and social theory. Thus, anything she says about sex will be found to be, not merely related to, but an integral part of all her other interests. In her notebooks we find this:

> In the *Symposium* and the *Phaedrus*, Plato seems to look upon chastity as a self-fertilisation on the part of man. Desire promotes the production of semen which instead of discharging itself exteriorly engenders a higher form of energy within himself.[9]

She goes on to observe that there is a misapprehension in the idea that artists need sexual freedom. It is true that they need some excitant so that their organism will produce the necessary energy for their art.

> But the satisfaction of the sexual instinct, far from assisting them, takes away from them a part of the energy thus developed. If they go on creating all the same, it is simply because they have a surplus amount of energy remaining over to them.[10]

And in her long essay, "Forms of the implicit love of God," she asserts that all men, from the noblest down to the most depraved, are aware that beauty is the only thing worthy of our love. "The words that express beauty come to the lips of all men when they want to praise the thing they love." And again in her essay on the *Timaeus* she observes that people use the word beautiful and its synonyms not only for their home town or countryside but also for all kinds of improbable things, such as machines. "Owing to the prevalent bad taste, the term is often badly misapplied by everybody including the cultured; but that is a different question. The point is that the word beauty speaks to every heart." [11] *

Physical love, in all its forms, including the most questionable, is in reality directed towards universal beauty, the beauty of the whole universe, and it is only by a kind of transference that it is fixed upon some particular object. "So it is a great error to reproach the mystics, as is sometimes done, for using the language of lovers. It is legitimately theirs, and others have only the right to borrow it."

These remarks are subsidiary to her main argument, and I quote them here only to show that as regards sex-repression it is not Simone Weil who is naive, but her critics. But while leaving aside the main argument we may look a little more closely at what she says about universal and particular love. No love is real unless it is directed towards a particular object, therefore the transference referred to above, from the universal to the particular, is obligatory and inevitable; and this brings us immediately to the tragic discovery that we cannot possess beauty by possessing the object in which we see it. Beauty is for looking at, not for eating. And, moreover, it is not an attribute of matter in itself. "It is a relation between the world and our sensibility, that sensibility which depends upon the structure of our body and soul." Obviously, you cannot eat a relation; and in trying to do so you merely unbalance it. But it is through repeated and fruitless attempts to do so—as Plato shows in the *Phaedrus*, by the image of the two horses, one docile and the other impetuous, of the chariot of the soul—that we learn in the end what beauty is.

> Perhaps vice, depravity, and crime are almost always, or even always, in their essence, attempts to eat beauty, to

* As is nicely illustrated in English by the expression "the beauty of it."

eat what we must only look at. Eve began it. If humanity was lost because she ate a fruit, then the opposite
attitude, looking at a fruit without eating it, should be
what saves humanity. "Two winged companions," says
an Upanishad, "two birds are on the branch of a tree.
One eats the fruit, the other looks at it." These two birds
are the two parts of the soul.[12]

They correspond to the two horses in the *Phaedrus,*
and in her essay on Plato Simone Weil concedes that
the violent and unruly horse who tries to hurl himself
upon the object of love is as much a help as a
hindrance. It is his violence that pulls the chariot
towards the good; and even his faults are useful,
because each of them initiates a further stage in his
training.

> The horse's temper may be very difficult and it may be a
> long time before there is any perceptible improvement;
> but it is absolutely certain that by being punished time
> after time he will become perfectly docile in the
> end. . . . The evil in us is finite, like ourselves. The
> good, with whose help we oppose it, is outside ourselves
> and is infinite.[13]

The grounds upon which Simone Weil based these
opinions will be considered in Part II. I have referred
to them here simply to show that they are similar to
Plato's and that if he was naïve about sex, then she was
too; and if not, not.

Either in 1941 or just before her departure for America
in 1942 Simone Weil wrote her two essays on the
civilisation of Languedoc. These essays might be
regarded as footnotes to her long essay on Hitler and
Rome, except that they represent independently and
in themselves a distinct and important element in her
thought. The theme of both these essays is that the

romanesque civilisation of Languedoc, Catalonia, and parts of Italy, in the twelfth century, held the promise of a renaissance far superior to the one which occurred three centuries later; and that the destruction of Languedoc by the crusade against the Albigensians early in the thirteenth century killed that promise and substituted for the Greek and Christian spirit, which was budding again in the romanesque civilisation, the imperialistic and totalitarian spirit of Rome.

Relying largely upon the second part of the contemporary Provençal text known as the *Song of the Crusade against the Albigensians*, and also of course upon the art and poetry and music of the period, she builds up what is no doubt an idealised picture of life in and around twelfth century Toulouse. But the virtues she attributes to it are genuinely historical in the sense that, however incompletely they may have been realised, they did in fact form part of the ethos of the romanesque civilisation: a social system imbued throughout with the spirit of feudal chivalry, and an intellectual tolerance which not only promoted peaceful coexistence between the orthodox Catholic and the Manichaean, or Cathar, or Albigensian traditions but was also open to Arabian, Persian, and other oriental influences. This corresponds, of course, very closely with Simone Weil's own idea of what civilisation should be. "Order can only exist," she wrote, "when the feeling for legitimate authority permits obedience without self-abasement." [14] The artisan and merchant classes in Languedoc, she thought, had the same sense of chivalry as the military class. Obedience in work was not something to be bought and sold, as in modern industrial society, but was the product of the civic feeling and sense of duty of free men. (Compare her 1934 essay on "The Causes of Liberty and Oppression.") And the poetry of the period, in Bernart de

Ventadour for example, occasionally touches heights "where its purity is comparable to that of Greek poetry." [15] All this was wiped out when the country was devastated and the Albigensians massacred by the armies of Simon de Montfort, sent against them by the Pope. Even the language of the country became obsolete, and the small-city civilisation of Languedoc was absorbed into the kingdom of France, which later became the aggressive, centralised Nation-State of Richelieu and Louis XIV.

It was not inevitable, she thought, that the decline of the feudal nobility in Europe and the rise of the bourgeoisie should involve the disappearance of the chivalric virtues, because in Languedoc these virtues were shared by the town folk. But—

> In the countries of the victors in this war it was quite otherwise; there was strife, not harmony, between the feudal spirit and the spirit of the towns. Between nobles and commoners there was a moral barrier. This was bound to produce what did, in fact, happen once the power of the nobility failed, namely the emergence of a class absolutely ignorant of the values of chivalry; a regime in which obedience became something to be bought and sold; the bitter class conflicts which necessarily go with an obedience divested of any sense of duty and maintained solely by the lowest motives. [16]

Such was the result of the Pope's victory over the Albigensians.

However far the cities of Languedoc may actually have fallen short of the ideals depicted in *The Song of the Crusade*, this scarcely affects the main argument of Simone Weil's two essays, which is: first, that the city-state, of which Greece and medieval Italy and, for a brief period, Languedoc provide the best examples, is more favourable to human creativity and happiness than the large, centralised Nation-State; and second, that it was the later Renaissance, and not the twelfth century one, that introduced into Europe the humanistic fallacy. This fallacy involved believing that the less good can give rise to the better, which implies that energy can be increased or upgraded when there is no external source of energy—a belief which neither science nor any authentic philosophy supports, and which leads ultimately to the absurd modern fallacy which she was to define later in her brilliant essay on Marxism as the belief that "matter is a machine for manufacturing good."

It is relevant to note here that in the other long essay she wrote in 1941–42 ("Forms of the Implicit Love of God") she instances one's mother tongue and one's city or native countryside as examples of the μεταξύ, things which, without being of absolute value in themselves, can serve as intermediaries between man and the absolute beauty which is the real object of his love. Thus it is a grave decision for a writer to decide to write in an acquired language, as Joseph Conrad did with a success which is an exception to the rule, and it is a grave responsibility to persuade a man to change his religion. It is clear that, for her, religious practices are on the level of μεταξύ.

One of Simone Weil's most striking characteristics was the absence in her of the faintest streak of chauvinism in any sphere whatsoever. (Unless, indeed, one could accuse her of a sort of negative chauvinism against ancient Rome and Hebraism.) As a passionate French patriot, who supported de Gaulle in the 1940's, one wonders what she would have thought and said about the idea of national "glory" which he propagated twenty years later. And her religious thought was equally unchauvinistic; her love of Christianity never caused her to speak, as most westerners do, as if the West were the holder of the world religious championship.

Nationalistic chauvinism at its worst, with its moth-eaten menagerie of bears, lions, eagles, cocks, bulldogs and whatnot, only appeared after Napoleon's destruction of the old European dynastic system; but in a very short time it spread far beyond Europe. We now take it so much for granted that we are scarcely conscious of the Nation-State as an unnatural and constricting influence which stifles culture and distorts or inhibits the exchange of thought across its frontiers. (The contemporary vogue of "tourism," so far from being a corrective, only emphasises the degree of our servitude.) Simone Weil, however, was acutely aware of it, and of what a recent malady it is. But her protests are probably unintelligible to readers who don't recognise it as a malady.

Religious chauvinism, on the other hand, is a very old and apparently incurable human weakness; and it persists even at times and places where religion itself is not taken seriously. It is remarkable, in view of this, that the comparatively recent European system of dating the events of world history as B.C. and A.D. should have been accepted without much protest by the chauvinists of other world religions; and the more so because it is an inconvenient system for historians of civilisation, of which our knowledge goes back at least three millennia before the birth of Christ. The only protest I have ever seen, and a very mild one, was from Nehru in the fascinating but intellectually shallow and, in Simone Weil's sense of the word, rootless account of world history which he wrote for his daughter while he was in prison. He there suggests that A.C. would be more suitable than A.D., in view of the fact that for Hindus, Buddhists, Jews, Mohammedans, and other non-Christians the word Dominus is not applicable, or is not exclusively applicable, to Christ.

Some westerners whose religious convictions are much shallower than Simone Weil's might find Nehru's suggestion disturbing, but there are many reasons for doubting whether it would have shocked her very much. In a letter to Jean Wahl, in 1942, she speaks of one identical thought, "expressed very precisely and with only very slight differences of modality," which is to be found in a whole series of religious and philosophical traditions, from the ancient mythologies and the Upanishads, through Pythagoras and Plato, to the dogmas of the Christian faith and the Cathar and Manichaean traditions. After which she adds:

> I believe that this thought is the truth, and that it requires today a modern and western form of expression. That is to say, it requires to be expressed through the only approximately good thing we can call our own, namely science. This is all the less difficult because it is itself the origin of science. There are a few texts which indicate with certainty that Greek geometry arose out of religious thought; and this thought appears to resemble Christianity almost to the point of identity.[17]

We shall return later to her views on the abject modern controversy between religion and science.

AS A JEWESS, Simone Weil was unable to teach under the Vichy government.[1] Her father, too, was prevented from working; and in May, 1942, she allowed herself to be persuaded to accompany her parents to New York. She had been nearly two years in the south of France, and except that she had assisted in the illegal distribution of the Resistance paper, *Témoignage chrétien,* her life does not seem to have been directly involved in the war. She would not have been herself if she had not worried lest the situation might become more dangerous after she left, in which case she foresaw that she would accuse herself of having run away. But she counted on getting from America to England, and she still believed she could persuade the army to adopt her scheme for frontline nurses. Alternatively, she hoped to persuade the Free French to employ her in sabotage missions and liaison with the European Resistance movements.

With these schemes in her head, it looks as if she was bent on getting herself killed in one way or another; and this is in strong contrast with the impression made by her Spanish journal of 1936. In Spain she had been interested to observe her own reactions to the danger of death, and she volunteered for any danger that offered, but she does not seem to have wanted to die, in fact quite the contrary. But in 1942 she is different. The danger of the Atlantic crossing seems to have been positively welcome. When someone referred to the risk of torpedoes, presumably with the hinted regret that she had not been baptised before facing the chance of death, she replied: "Don't you think the sea would make a fine baptistry?" [2]

And yet her brain was still teeming with ideas for work. One of them was for a collaboration with Father Perrin in collecting pre-Christian and non-Christian texts illustrative of implicit Christian thought. She was also engaged in a comprehensive study of mythology and folklore from an immense range of sources and languages, including Sanskrit; and her notebooks for 1941–43 contain the fragmentary material for what could have been a kind of twentieth-century *Summa* of scientific and religious thought, revealing the essential identity of the two, which was, she maintained, understood by the Greeks and has been completely forgotten since the Renaissance.

Once in America, she immediately began to seek a way of getting back across the Atlantic to London, and thanks, it would seem, chiefly to André Philip and Maurice Schumann, she finally achieved her wish, sailing from New York to Liverpool on November 10, 1942. While in New York, she met a number of Frenchmen in exile who spoke abusively of the Vichy government's supporters; and she herself had every reason to dislike a government which not only represented surrender to Hitler but had also reduced her to a second-class citizen and debarred her from teaching. But she characteristically resented the unimaginative and censorious attitude of those who, from a safe distance of three thousand miles, uttered blanket condemnations against their "collaborating" fellow countrymen. Since most people are incapable of understanding fairness of mind (which Simone Weil herself was capable of extending not only to Pétain but also, as we shall see, to Hitler) this led to rumours that she was a Vichy sympathiser. Writing to Jean Wahl from New York, she explains herself as follows:

> What may have given rise to such rumours is the fact that I don't much like to hear perfectly comfortable people here using words like coward and traitor about people in France who are managing as best they can in a terrible situation. . . . The word traitor should only be used about those of whom one feels certain that they desire Germany's victory and are doing what they can to that end. As for the others, some of those who are prepared to work with Vichy or even with the Germans may have honourable motives which are justified by particular situations. And others may be constrained by pressures which they could only resist if they were heroes. Most of the people here, however, who set themselves up as judges have never had an opportunity to find out if they themselves are heroes. I detest facile, unjust, and false attitudes, and especially when the pressure of public opinion seems to make them almost obligatory.[3]

Simone Weil worked for four months in London until, in April, 1943, she was admitted to the Middlesex Hospital with pulmonary tuberculosis. If all the work she completed in London was also begun there the amount would be prodigious. It includes a book (*The Need for Roots*), two long essays ("Human Personality" and "Is There a Marxist Doctrine?"), an essay on the colonial problem, many pages of notes, and a considerable number of pieces written especially for the Free French organisation. No doubt some of this work consisted in putting into shape notes and articles that were already partly written, but even so it is a remarkable output, and very much more so when one considers its unique and extraordinary value and also the fact that she was in great mental distress the whole time and was not eating enough (because she felt she ought not to eat more than the civilian rations in German-occupied France). She was in distress because, although she was treated with great consideration as an intellectual colleague and given an almost free hand to write what she liked, it soon became clear that both her nursing scheme and her request to be used for sabotage and liaison with the Resistance would be turned down.

In the series of letters [4] she wrote to her parents who were still in New York she touches lightly on her disappointment (which must have been the opposite to them!) and says nothing about her deteriorating health. These letters are interesting in themselves for many reasons; they give the impressions of a French intellectual on her first visit to England and seeing it at a uniquely exceptional time. Her view of England, both in these letters and in most of her references to it in her essays, may strike some English readers as being appreciative to the point of indulgence. But she approached the country with favourable preconceptions because she considered that, compared with other countries, it was somewhat less deracinated from the Christian past and therefore a little less corrupted by the vices of the modern Nation-State.[5] But what makes this correspondence almost unbearably poignant, as well as beautiful, is the way she assumes an air of cheerfulness and enjoyment and urges her parents to make the most of any pleasures they can get in New York—at a time when she herself was *literally* dying of chagrin. To prevent them from knowing that she was ill she continued, when she wrote to them from the Middlesex Hospital, to use the address of her lodgings.

She had made great friends with her landlady (the poor widow who was to be one of the seven mourners at her funeral) and had taken her youngest boy to be treated for thyroid at the infirmary of the French Headquarters.

It is also touching to see how thirstily she drank every drop of beauty that London could offer in the wartime spring of 1943. The early-flowering fruit trees, whose blossom is the more beautiful because it not only is but also appears to be so frail and fleeting, had always been one of her symbols for the precariousness of happiness in the world; and she was quick to notice, what so many Londoners never seem to see, the extreme beauty of the first almond blossom, which makes its appearance in the parks and squares as early as February, while every other tree is still bare. On March 1 she tells her parents: "There are trees of pink blossom in the London squares. London is full of delicious little squares." And on April 17: "London is full of pink and white blossoming trees." And on May 10: "Fruit blossom of every kind is full out."

They were the last spring flowers she was ever to see. In August she was moved from London to a sanatorium near Ashford, where she died.

The *Kentish Express* of 3 September, 1943, carried the report of an inquest at Ashford on Professor Simone A. Weil, 34, late of the University of Paris. It was headed "Strange Suicide. Refused to eat," and it reported the evidence of a woman doctor, the senior medical officer at the Grosvenor Sanatorium, Kennington, Ashford, who said:

> She tried to persuade Professor Weil to take some food and she said she would try. She did not eat, however, and gave as a reason the thought of her people in France

starving. She died on August 24 and death was due to cardiac failure due to degeneration through starvation.

She was pronounced to have committed suicide by starvation "while the balance of her mind was disturbed."

To judge the balance of a mind is a delicate operation. Can we be sure that what is called a well-balanced mind is not in reality unbalanced on the side of inertia, self-deception, and self-interest? If that should be the case, then the law of equilibrium, in which Simone Weil was greatly interested, would require a mind to be very far out on the other side to balance all the millions of "well-balanced" minds. However, it was certainly a strange death, after a strange life, even though the effect of strangeness was due, as I believe, to an abnormally refined sense of balance. But before giving my reasons I must examine a piece of evidence which, to some readers, might seem to point the other way. This is the long letter written in London, probably at the end of January or early February, to Maurice Schumann.[6] It is a last desperate appeal to him for help in procuring for her some mission that would fulfill her need to experience hardship and danger. She had already written to him a few months earlier from New York [7] explaining her state of mind—"which luckily is not shared by everybody," she admits, "because it would make organised action impossible." But the suffering in the world, she continues, obsesses her to the point of destroying her faculties, and she can only revive them and cure the obsession if she herself has a large share of suffering and danger.

> I beseech you to get for me, if you can, the necessary amount of suffering and danger to save me from being wasted by chagrin.

In considering her two letters to Schumann one needs
to remember that they are among the very few letters
she ever wrote where she talks about herself. Usually
what she writes about moral problems is intended to
be of universal application, but here she is writing
about her own personal problem and she admits she is
a special case. It is therefore quite beside the point to
make the criticism so often applied to mystics—what
would happen if everybody behaved in the same way?
She was so far from recommending herself as an
example that at the same time that she was writing
these letters she was also writing *The Need for Roots*,
which could be described as an investigation into the
causes of unhappiness in society and a prescription for
its cure. We shall have to consider later whether it was
illogical to prescribe happiness for other people and
suffering for herself, but for the present we will only
look at two striking passages in her last letter to
Schumann.

She says that her temperament and her headaches
have reduced her "by a purely mechanical and therefore valueless process" to a state of detachment and
denudation similar to that of the saints. But in her case
it is rather that of a slave:

> circumstances having automatically put into my hands
> this ersatz of sanctity I feel the perfectly clear obligation
> to make it my rule of life, although it is valueless,
> uniquely out of love for the genuine article. Not in the
> hope of acquiring it, but simply to pay it
> homage. . . . If I stay rigorously faithful to it, I am still
> far below those who, possessing an intact life, full of sap
> and normal aspirations for happiness, expend even a tiny
> bit of it for the sake of justice and truth.

In view of the fact that, when her headaches per-
mitted, Simone Weil was capable of an extreme and
intense enjoyment of life this statement seems exagger-

ated. But it needs to be read alongside another passage in the same letter:

> I feel an ever increasing sense of devastation, both in my intellect and in the centre of my heart, at my inability to think with truth at the same time about the affliction of men, the perfection of God, and the link between the two.
>
> I have the inner certainty that this truth, if it is ever granted to me, will only be revealed when I myself am physically in affliction, and in one of the extreme forms in which it exists at present.
>
> I am afraid it may not happen. Even as a child and when I thought myself an atheist and a materialist, I always had the fear of failing, not in my life, but in my death.

Her joy in life, and also her physical suffering, had culminated in the experience of 1938, which gave her direct and unmediated knowledge of the existence, somewhere outside the universe as known to human faculties, of an infinite and perfect love—which is what she means by "the perfection of God"; and this knowledge existed alongside her knowledge of the horror of life in the universe. How this problem affected her thought, we shall see. How it affected her life, we have already seen; and it is difficult to describe the effect on her life except by saying that it made her want to die. Or if that is saying too much, it at least made her adopt a course of behaviour which can only be described, objectively, as suicidal. Subjectively, she herself may have regarded the virtual certainty of death as incidental, like that of someone who refuses to get into a lifeboat for fear of overweighting it, and not for the sake of being drowned. But it seems almost certain that with a part of her mind, at any rate, she welcomed the prospect of death.

She was young, she was brilliantly gifted, her brain was teeming with ideas for work; and she loved the world and the people in it, so that, in a sense, she loved life. So why should she want to die? I do not believe that there is any simple answer, such as that she had not learned to live with her genius, though that may be true, so far as it goes, and one may legitimately regret, from one point of view, that she did not live long enough to develop the gift for self-protective relaxation which genius sometimes acquires and which comes so easily to mediocrity. But I believe there is a much more true and complete answer, though it is very difficult to put into a phrase. One way of putting it would be to say that she wanted to die for the good of her soul.

This answer is certainly true, but it is also strange when one remembers that she was totally unconcerned as to whether her soul would survive her, and thought it unlikely. Or so I deduce from passages like the following, the first from her notebooks of 1942–43 and the second from a letter of 1937:

> The Last Judgement will be like this. — The soul which has just passed through what men call death becomes suddenly, irresistibly, convinced beyond all possibility of doubt that *all the ends,* including God, towards which its actions were directed during life, were illusions. Entirely penetrated in all its parts, including the sensibility, by this certainty, it reviews in thought all the actions of its life.
>
> After which, in most cases, it is seized with horror, longs to be annihilated, and disappears.
>
> There are rare cases where nothing is regretted, or where at least the soul can fix on some actions which it does not regret, because they were unconditional, they were acts of pure obedience.
>
> It is not seized with horror, but continues to be oriented, with love, towards the good.
>
> However, it feels its personality as a barrier which hinders its perfect contact with the good; desires it to be dissolved; and disappears.
>
> Perhaps one single act of pure, unreserved obedience

is enough. But if there has been one, there will have been many.[8]

In 1937 she had written to Jean Posternak:

The problem of a future after death can have no effect upon the data of any real problem in life. The problem is to raise oneself in this life to the level of eternal things (mens sentit experiturque se aeternam esse, said Spinoza), by struggling free from bondage to what is perpetually renewed and destroyed. And if everything disappears when we die, it is all the more important not to bungle this life which is given us, but to manage to have saved one's soul before it disappears. I am convinced that this is the real thought of Socrates and Plato (as also of the Gospel) and that all the rest is only symbols and metaphors.[9]

She did not, in any case, think of her soul as "her own," and whether or not she thought it would survive the dissolution of her personality she would not have considered that what survived was in any sense "herself." And indeed it would be morbidly self-centred to be so interested in one's soul if one regarded it as "one's own." But in Simone Weil's case the good of her soul demanded throughout her life a continual, unremitting effort for the good of other people and a ruthless neglect of herself. Then why did she want to cut the effort short by death? One possible answer is that she felt called upon to bear witness to something, and that she believed—whether rightly or wrongly it would be very presumptuous to judge—that her death would bear more effective witness to it than her life. But this is not to say that she wanted to be a martyr. On the contrary, she thought martyrdom was too much associated with illusions of triumph and sometimes also with self-satisfaction. And if one had asked her how an obscure death, without the halo of martyrdom, could bear witness to anything, since so few people would even hear about it, she would have replied, I think, that truth comes by stealth, that it is not propagated by advertisement, and that it is not statistical. The grain of mustard seed is the smallest of all seeds.

She wrote, in the last year of her life, that "a single thought of love, lifted up to God in truthfulness, even though mute and without echo, is more useful, even for this world, than the most splendid action," [10] but whatever she may have meant by this it seems reasonable to believe that she hoped that both her life and her death would be useful in bearing witness to a truth of which she felt certain and of which she felt the world was desperately in need.

In what sense, if at all, was her death a tragedy? It was a great public loss in the sense that it deprived the world of what she might have done in later years. But, in another sense, it is stupid to speak of tragedy in connection with a woman who could write in her private journal:

> Perfect and infinite joy really exists in God. My participation can add nothing, my non-participation can take away nothing from the reality of this perfect and infinite joy. Of what importance is it then whether I am to share in it or not? Of no importance whatever. [11]

By ordinary standards, however, there is something tragic about her death, and the best consolation one can find for it was well expressed by Raymond Rosenthal in a review in *The New Leader* in which he said that her special genius "was to show that private suffering can have a vital public, social value." [12] It is also true, however, that she died as a witness, though not as a martyr, to her faith; and it is to her faith and the reasons she gave for holding it that we must now turn our attention.

PART II

The Angel that presided o'er my birth
Said "Little creature, form'd of joy and mirth,
Go, love without the help of anything on earth."
—WILLIAM BLAKE, Gnomic Verses

ALTHOUGH SIMONE WEIL was a professional philosopher, nearly everything she wrote for publication was written in nontechnical language intelligible to the general reader; and her notebooks and letters, too, except when she writes about mathematics and science, are usually written in straightforward nontechnical French. My problem in attempting to summarise her thought, therefore, is not so much technical as literary—how to condense into a hundred pages the ideas about life and human nature and the destiny of man which are scattered through more than a dozen volumes compiled after her death by editors who could only guess how she herself would have wished to arrange them.

If we call a thinker original we mean, or should mean, that his way of thinking is original, not his thoughts. People will always be thinking up new intellectual gimmicks, of course, but how could any man have a radically new thought which had never occurred to anyone else before? (If we flatter ourselves that nevertheless we know a lot more than our ancestors did, T. S. Eliot's comment is the right one: We do indeed know more than they did, and *they* are the more that we know.) Philosophically speaking, Simone Weil's thought derives very largely from Plato; but having said this one has said very little. She was an extraordinarily original thinker, and I shall try to present her ideas, so far as I can understand them, not as a system but as a myth or "likely story," as Plato called his myths. One can find a starting point almost anywhere in her work because, to quote Mr. Rosenthal again, she possessed in a high degree "that marvellous ability, found only in the greatest thinkers, to reflect the whole of her work in each of its parts." [1] We may begin, then, with the essay "Is There a Marxist Doctrine?" which she wrote in London in 1943 and left unfinished. In this essay she describes materialism as one of the inferior forms of the religious life. The genuine religious life, she says, consists in facing the absolute contradiction between justice and force, the infinite distance between the good and the necessary. And her definition of true philosophy is similar: philosophy consists in posing the insoluble problems and facing them in their insolubility, contemplating them in humility, without hope, indefinitely.

> The essential contradiction in human life is that man, whose very being consists in an effort towards the good, is at the same time subject in his entire being, both in his thinking and his flesh, to a blind force, to a necessity completely indifferent to the good. So it is; and that is why no human thinking can escape from contradiction. It is by no means always that contradiction is a criterion of error; it is sometimes a sign of truth. Plato knew this. But the cases can be distinguished. There is a legitimate and an illegitimate use of contradiction.
>
> The illegitimate use consists in coupling together incompatible thoughts as if they were compatible. [2]

This is what the inferior forms of religion do, and it is what materialism does. Since man cannot face being alone with his longing for good in a universe ruled by force and necessity, since he feels too weak to be able "to love without the help of anything on earth," he seeks an all-powerful ally, and if he is a materialist he finds this ally in omnipotent matter. Dialectical materialists, creative evolutionists, atheist humanists, and other materialist thinkers, having no conception of mysticism, find themselves obliged to conceive matter as a machine for manufacturing good. Thus Marx, for example, conceived history "as though he attributed to matter what is the very essence of mind—an unceasing aspiration towards the best." It is believed, therefore, that while omnipotent matter "rolls on its relentless way" (to quote the well-known purple passage of a famous modern materialist) it somehow happens, somewhere along the line, that goodness, beauty, justice and all the so-called human values are evolved.

This belief, says Simone Weil, is an example of the illegitimate use of contradiction.

> As Plato said, an infinite distance separates the good from necessity. They have nothing in common. They are totally other. Although we are forced to assign them a unity, this unity is a mystery; it remains for us a secret. The authentic religious life is the contemplation of this unknown unity.
>
> The manufacture of a fictitious, mistaken equivalent of this unity, so as to make it accessible to human faculties, is the basis of the inferior forms of the religious life. To every genuine form of the religious life there corresponds an inferior form, which is based to all appearances on the same doctrine, but has no understanding of it. . . . In this respect the whole of materialism, in so far as it attributes to matter the automatic manufacture of the good, is to be classed among the inferior forms of the religious life.[3]

To believe the fiction that matter automatically produces something better than itself is to believe that the less good creates the better, which is equivalent to believing that low-grade energy can be transformed into high-grade without a corresponding transformation of high-grade energy into low-grade.[4]

So justice, beauty, and love cannot be products of "omnipotent matter." Nevertheless, their names are often given to things which are such products: justice, for example. What we call justice is usually no more than the compromise between two forces of which neither is strong enough to destroy the other. It is simply an index of the relation of forces at any given moment. And yet there *is* such a thing as true justice and it is sometimes, though very rarely, seen in the world. There is true justice when a man in a position of strength behaves towards a man in a position of weakness exactly as he would do if the balance of force between them was equal. But this is against nature. Everything in nature always exerts all the force at its disposal and when it meets with another force it either crushes it, compromises with it, or is crushed by it, according to its relative strength. True justice, therefore, is supernatural; it belongs to a different order of reality from the world of science, the world accessible to our minds, or to our senses, or to the instruments by which we amplify our senses.

To accuse Simone Weil of maligning human nature and to appeal to the many examples of behaviour in civilised life which seem to contradict the rule of self-assertion and force is to be self-deceived. A human being is not a single unanimous force but a compound of dissonant forces, and his behaviour is their resultant. Among the forces in him which may produce the false semblance of an act of justice are the desire for self-esteem, or for social approbation, or for a quid pro quo, or for a "reward in heaven," or for the pleasure of receiving gratitude. There is nothing extraordinary, says Simone Weil, in the fact that someone who has plenty of bread should give a piece to a starving man. But if he gives it in an unmercenary spirit then his behaviour is more than extraordinary, it is supernatural. "Almsgiving, unless it is supernatural, is like a commercial transaction. It is a way of purchasing the victim of misfortune." [5]

It is against nature for the strong to identify himself imaginatively with the weak, whereas it is natural for the weak to feel sympathy for the strong, because by identifying himself with the strong he acquires an imaginary strength.

> That is why the sympathy of the weak for the strong is only pure if its sole object is the sympathy received from the other, when the other is truly generous. This is supernatural gratitude, which means being glad to be the recipient of supernatural compassion. It leaves self-respect absolutely intact. The preservation of true self-respect in affliction is also something supernatural. Gratitude which is pure, like pure compassion, is essentially the acceptance of affliction. The afflicted man and his benefactor, between whom diversity of fortune places an infinite distance, are united in this acceptance. There is friendship between them in the sense of the Pythagoreans, miraculous harmony and equality.
>
> Both of them recognise at the same time, with all their soul, that it is better not to command wherever one has the power to do so. If this thought fills the whole soul and controls the imagination, which is the source of our actions, it constitutes true faith. For it places the good outside this world, which contains all the sources of power; it recognises it as the archetype of the secret point which lies at the centre of human personality and which is the principle of renunciation.
>
> Even in science and art, though second-class work, brilliant or mediocre, is an extension of the self, work of the very highest order, true creation, is self-renunciation. . . . Love for our neighbour, being made of creative attention, is analogous to genius.[6]

This difficult passage contains a number of Simone Weil's key ideas, but the one which concerns us here is the idea that true justice "places the good outside this world."

All true justice, all true love, and all true beauty, she maintains, always point to somewhere outside this world. In the last analysis, all love is love of beauty, which is, in fact, "the only universally recognised value"; [7] and beauty is not an object in the world at all. The beauty of human beings, flowers, music, or landscape is not something intrinsic to the human body and mind, or to vegetable matter, sound, colour, and so on. As we have seen in her comments on the *Phaedrus*, Simone Weil defines beauty as a relation between our sensibility and the surrounding world. If our sensibility were different, our conception of beauty would be different. But whatever our conception of beauty may be, it always leads to frustration.

> Beauty always promises but never gives anything; it stimulates hunger but has no nourishment for the part of the soul which looks in this world for sustenance. It feeds only the part of the soul which gazes. [8]

As an introduction to Simone Weil's thought the preceding account is inevitably distorted by oversimplification and compression, but it should at least make clear that although her view of life is essentially tragic she gives a central place to desire, joy, and love of beauty. A great part of her work consists of a ruthless demonstration that human behaviour, in history, in modern society, among artists, scientists, politicians, and ordinary men and women of all classes, is very often no more than a self-deceiving effort to find substitutes for the real desire of the soul and to disguise the fact that nothing "here below," as she puts it—nothing, that is to say, in the world of force and material necessity—can ever assuage the soul's hunger. But it is not cynicism or misanthropy that inspire her analyses. On the contrary, her motive is to protest against the universal tendency to accept stones in place of the bread for which the soul insatiably hungers, and which is unobtainable here below. As described by her, a human being is simply an incarnation of desire, of hunger for the good, and this hunger is the only fact that gives value or meaning to his life. Without it his individual life is as mechanical as the individual waves which undulate, in obedience to the laws of hydrome-chanics, on the surface of the sea; and his death has no more meaning than the subsidence of a wave. All that happens is that a form is dissolved, to be replaced by other similar forms composed of the same constituent material.

But the human material is distinguished by a myste-rious property; it is infused with an insatiable, though often blind and hardly conscious, desire for good; and however this good may be conceived, it is always as some sort of approximation to perfect beauty. And the lesson that men have to learn is that beauty is for looking at and not for eating. "It stimulates hunger but has no nourishment for the part of the soul which looks in this world for sustenance."

It is obvious that anyone who believes all this and takes it seriously, and who refuses to drug himself with imaginary consolations, will suffer and perhaps fall into despair. But that, for Simone Weil, is precisely the vocation of the philosopher and also, if I have rightly understood her, of the Christian. And she believed that to anyone who is prepared to endure the suffering indefinitely, with humility and lucidity, sooner or later something will happen, as it happened to her. We already know what happened to her in 1938; and it was certainly upon the strength of that experience that she wrote, in 1943, what she called her "profession of faith."

This crucial text forms the first part of the "Draft for a Statement of Human Obligations" which appears to be, like her book, *The Need for Roots* (which is an amplification of the same thesis and is subtitled "Prelude to a Declaration of Duties Towards Mankind"), one of the memoranda she wrote for the Free French in London in connexion with postwar policy. It appears to me to be an attempt to express in formal and general terms the personal experience of 1938 which she seems to have mentioned to nobody except Father Perrin and Joë Bousquet and which she described to the former in the words: "Christ himself came down and took possession of me." It is therefore a statement of central importance for the understanding of her work. It does not, however, follow that if anyone finds it unintelligible he will have the same difficulty with the rest of her work. She herself, indeed, in a passage of *La Connaissance surnaturelle* (written in 1942–43) to which I shall return, raises the question of whether it would alter her behaviour or her opinions if she believed that God was an illusion, and she gives satisfactory reasons for deciding that it would not. The word 'God' in fact nowhere occurs in her profession of faith, nor does the word 'supernatural'; but what does occur repeatedly is the word 'reality,' applied to something independent of time and space and absolutely beyond the reach of human faculties. Here are the first five paragraphs of the statement:

> There is a reality outside the world, that is to say, outside space and time, outside man's mental universe, outside any sphere whatsoever that is accessible to human faculties.
>
> Corresponding to this reality, at the centre of the human heart, is the longing for an absolute good, a longing which is always there and is never appeased by any object in this world.
>
> Another terrestrial manifestation of this reality lies in the absurd and insoluble contradictions which are always the terminus of human thought when it moves exclusively in this world.

Just as the reality of this world is the sole foundation of facts, so that other reality is the sole foundation of good.

That reality is the unique source of all the good that can exist in this world: that is to say, all beauty, all truth, all justice, all legitimacy, all order, and all human behaviour that is mindful of obligations.[9]

A reader who has followed my account of Simone Weil thus far with sympathy is not likely to find much to quarrel with in this passage. As regards the third paragraph, she observes elsewhere that it is the paradoxical, the contradictory, that is the test of the real: "When through clear conception one is brought up against the inconceivable, that is the shock produced by reality." [10] (The same thought is expressed by Goethe in his maxim that "Man is only really thinking when the object of his thought is something which he cannot think out to a conclusion.") And as regards the fifth paragraph, her reason for emphasising legitimacy, order, and obligations (but not rights) is made clear in *The Need for Roots*, which will be the subject of the next chapter. The sixth paragraph, however, does seem to present a difficulty. It is this:

Those minds whose attention and love are turned towards that reality are the sole intermediary through which good can descend from there and come among men.

What makes this difficult is the fact that in the immediately preceding paragraph the very first example she gives of the good, which comes into the world from outside the sphere of reality known to us, is beauty. It is not immediately obvious why beauty and our joy in it—for Simone Weil, for example, the beauty of almond blossom or of "the smile on a beloved face"—should require the intermediary of a mind whose attention and love are turned towards the "other reality." But since she defines beauty as a relation between our sensibility and some external object and as having, so far as the reality of this world is concerned, no purpose beyond itself ("It stimulates hunger but has no nourishment for the part of the soul which looks in this world for sustenance"), she presumably means that when this relation exists for a man it is a proof that his mind is, at least temporarily, attending to the other reality.

In a subsequent paragraph it is asserted that although this reality is beyond the reach of any human faculties man's power of turning towards it with attention and love depends solely upon his consent to do so; and although she does not say so here she often speaks as if she conceived of this consent as being difficult to give and likely to lead to a prolonged ordeal of suffering and endurance. And here we are brought up against an apparent contradiction. Simone Weil frequently quoted Aeschylus' "learning through suffering," and it is a common and on the whole a plausible criticism of her that she was masochistically obsessed with the necessity of suffering. Yet on the other hand she insists again and again that joy, if it is extreme and unmixed, is equivalent to suffering as a means of enlightenment; * and in her social and political essays she takes it for granted that the aim of politics and

* For example, "Before one can hear the divine silence, one needs to have been compelled to seek in vain for a finality in this world, and there are only two things which have the power to compel us: either affliction, or else that pure joy which comes from the feeling of beauty. Beauty possesses this power because, although it contains no particular finality, it irresistibly imposes a sense of some finality. Affliction and joy which is pure and extreme are the only two ways, and they are equivalent; but affliction is Christ's way." (*Intuitions pré-chrétiennes*, p. 168.) By "the feeling for beauty" she does not, of course, mean merely aesthetic connoisseurship; she means what a man feels for his familiar countryside, the faces he loves, his language and traditions, everything that gives beauty to his life. She accuses of sacrilege those aesthetes who reduce beauty to a luxurious toy.

social organisation should be to promote happiness. In the very essay which we are now studying she goes on to enumerate the needs of the human soul, and concludes as follows:

> Any place where the needs of human beings are satisfied can be recognised by the fact that there is a flowering of fraternity, joy, beauty, and happiness. Wherever people are lonely and turned in on themselves, wherever there is sadness or ugliness, there are privations that need remedying.[11]

The paragraph in her profession of faith which suggests that she is trying to express in formal and general terms her own experience of 1938 is the following:

> To anyone who does actually consent to directing his attention and love beyond the world, towards the reality that exists outside the reach of all human faculties, it is given to succeed in doing so. In that case, sooner or later, there descends upon him a part of the good, which shines through him upon all that surrounds him.[12]

This appears to be an impersonal way of describing the experience that "Christ himself came down and took possession of me"; and it shows that she believed that the same experience is possible for everybody. "All human beings," she says on the same page, "are absolutely identical in so far as they can be thought of as consisting of a centre, which is an unquenchable desire for good, surrounded by an accretion of psychical and bodily matter."

To students of mysticism, or to professional theologians and philosophers, Simone Weil's profession of faith might, I suppose, provide themes for academic discussion; but she undoubtedly wrote it for the plain reader, and the plain reader is all too likely to react in one or the other of two ways: either he will say that she was self-deceived, or else he will say that she was a saint or a special case, that her standards were too high, and that her ideas are irrelevant for ordinary people. I shall argue in the next chapter that her ideas are anything but irrelevant for ordinary people; but this is perhaps the place to meet the other reaction, by pointing out that Simone Weil herself was prepared to face, and was unshaken by, the possibility that she might be self-deceived. In *La Connaissance surnaturelle*, which consists of her notebooks of 1942 and 1943, there is the following note.

> If we put obedience to God above everything else, unreservedly, with the following thought: "Suppose God is real, then our gain is total even though we fall into nothingness at the moment of death; suppose the word 'God' stands only for illusions, then we have still lost nothing because on this supposition there is absolutely nothing good, and consequently nothing to lose; we have even gained, through being in accord with truth, because we have left aside the illusory goods which exist but are not good for the sake of something which (on this supposition) does not exist but which, if it did exist, would be the only good ... "
>
> If one follows this rule of life, then no revelation at the moment of death can cause any regrets; because if chance or the devil govern all worlds one would still have no regrets for having lived in this way.[13]

We note that in either case, whether God exists or not, the question of whether she herself will disappear into nothingness when she dies is a matter of indifference to her. And as for the existence or nonexistence of God:

> If God should be an illusion from the point of view of existence, He is the sole reality from the point of view of the good. I know that for certain, because it is a definition. "God is the good" is as certain as "I am."[14]

Therefore one is in accord with the truth in directing one's whole desire solely towards the good "without knowing whether it exists or not." This point of view, she claims, is greatly preferable to Pascal's famous wager. And indeed it obviously is, both intellectually and morally.

But of course Simone Weil knew very well that the good exists. Her mystical experience gave her, no doubt, a peculiar certainty; but several years earlier, when she was working in factories in 1934–35, she already knew quite as well as when she was writing *La Connaissance surnaturelle*, that a place where "there is a flowering of fraternity, joy, beauty, and happiness," because human needs are satisfied there, is better than a place where "people are lonely and turned in on themselves" because their souls are starved. Her originality is in her analysis of the needs of human beings, which is the implicit subject of most of her work and is set forth explicitly in her "Draft for a Statement of Human Obligations" and in *The Need for Roots*. And, as will be seen in the next chapter, it is precisely because her morality is more clearheaded that her views on social organisation are more hardheaded than those of our contemporary liberal humanists and idealistic progressives.

To put her social thought in the right perspective we may glance at a passage in one of her essays of 1943, where she concedes that mysticism is by its very nature a minority phenomenon but insists that society can and must be constellated around it. "Everything that is not directly in contact with it should be, as it were, impregnated by it through the mediation of beauty. This very nearly came to pass in the Romanesque Middle Ages, that amazing epoch when men's eyes and ears were refreshed every day by a beauty which was perfect in simplicity and purity." [15] A society which has lost all contact with the supernatural, or the "other reality," must inevitably degenerate into a specimen of the "social beast" as described by Plato in the *Republic*, a collective animal entirely governed by the blind forces of social mechanics. That is how she saw the Roman Empire; and that is what she thought modern Western society is becoming, thanks to the intellectual degeneracy which has produced the dichotomy between religion and science. In another of her essays of 1943 we find this:

> If we examine closely not only the Middle Ages of Christendom, but all the really creative civilisations, we notice how each one, at any rate for a time, had at its very centre an empty space reserved for the purely supernatural, the reality that lies outside this world. Everything else was oriented towards this empty space.
>
> There are not two methods of social architecture. There has never been more than one. It is eternal. But it is always the eternal which calls for a truly inventive effort on the part of the human spirit. This consists of disposing the blind forces of social mechanics around the point that also serves as centre for the blind forces of celestial mechanics, that is to say the "Love which moves the sun and the other stars." . . . Today, after being bemused for several centuries with pride in technical achievement, we have forgotten the existence of a divine order of the universe. We do not realise that labour, art, and science are only different ways of entering into contact with it.
>
> If the humiliation produced by unhappiness were to rouse us, if we were to re-discover this great truth, we should be able to put an end to what constitutes the scandal of modern thought, the hostility between religion and science.[16]

The whole effort of all of the most valuable thinkers of the twentieth century has been against the stream of modern thought, which has been flooded for two centuries and more by a spate of humanistic and evolutionary philosophies. These philosophies have always propagated in one form or another the belief that matter is a machine for manufacturing good, or in other words that man is self-sufficient and has created his own values *ex nihilo*. It would be difficult to name any thinker of this century who has exposed this fallacy more convincingly or analysed its consequences more penetratingly than Simone Weil has done.

The explosive power of a book like *The Need for Roots* lies in its combination of idealism with realism. Simone Weil is convinced that force is absolutely sovereign "here below," and that every attempt to derive our idea of justice from the world that is revealed to us by the intellect is a sentimental fraud. But she also knows that justice is not unreal. "We know this experimentally. Justice is real in men's hearts. Among the realities of this universe the structure of a human heart possesses as much title to reality as the trajectory of a planet." [17] Therefore the universe as seen from here below is not the whole universe. There is another reality besides the one to which we are in bondage. The difficulty of conceiving truthfully the two realities and the link between them was experienced by Simone Weil, as she wrote to Maurice Schumann, with "an ever increasing sense of devastation, both in my intellect and in the centre of my heart"; and this, in addition to her desire to bear witness to her faith, might be another possible explanation of her death.

To wear herself out in the contemplation of an insoluble contradiction would be, according to her theory, an appropriate death for a philosopher. But there is yet a third possible explanation of her death, which is that she had anticipated her own picture of the Last Judgement. It will be remembered that according to this picture the soul, even if it is not seized with horror on reviewing its past life, nevertheless "feels its personality as a barrier which hinders its perfect contact with the good; desires it to be dissolved; and disappears."

WHEN GUSTAVE THIBON criticised a certain stiffness in her literary style, Simone Weil admitted that this was a fault, but added that of all faults it was the least displeasing to her because there is a touch of it in most of the art that she particularly loved; Giotto, Gregorian music, romanesque and early fifth century Greek sculpture, and in general the art that comes a little before a period of classical maturity. It may be that M. Thibon's point is the aesthetic equivalent of the criticism expressed by T. S. Eliot in religious terms in his preface to *The Need for Roots:* "In the Church there is much to which she is blind, or about which she is strangely silent: she seems to give no thought to the Blessed Virgin." And I believe the same point can be put in psychological terms by saying that Simone Weil, with all her admiration for St Francis, was deficient in some of the most typical Franciscan characteristics. It is true that she writes a lot about beauty in general terms, as "the beauty of the world"; but she seldom descends to particulars, and among her very few references to animals I can only remember one which shows any interest in them. This is where she says that children are unlikely to believe our morality is sincere when they see the callousness with which we kill animals for food.[1]

Nevertheless, she certainly was not cold or impersonal, but quite the contrary. She is an illustration of the truth that it is those who are liable to be carried away by their feelings who best understand the need for disciplining them; just as it is only those who are gifted with personality who can see it, as she did, as an obstacle and a burden.

The term 'intellectual' has become devalued in our time to the point where it is almost insulting to apply it to anyone; but, using the word in its best sense, one could say that Simone Weil was intellectual to an extreme degree. She therefore inevitably possessed the defects of the quality. This means that she had in some ways less affinity with St Francis, whom she loved, than with St Augustine and Pascal and some others for whom her feelings were lukewarm. To regret this would be as absurd as to regret the lack of romanticism in a classical artist, or vice versa; but it remains true that an occasional relaxation of her unvarying seriousness would be welcome. She knew very well that perfect detachment means being detached even from one's detachment, but her writing hardly shows it.

However, to call a person an intellectual is not an adequate description, and it goes only a very little way towards describing Simone Weil. To begin with, she was an intellectual who believed that genius means humility in the sphere of thought, which is the last thing one would look for in contemporary intellectuals and is, indeed, scarcely compatible with the assumptions of evolutionary humanism. She had neither the grotesque sense of superiority nor the remoteness from common people which are so usual among intellectuals today. She was an intellectual who worked alongside factory hands and peasants because she wanted to experience their problems before working out her ideas for increasing their happiness; and but for her example one might fail to notice how extraordinary it is that revolutionaries and reformers should never see the need for this. It is true of course that some revolutionaries and reformers have come from the manual working class; but they have scarcely ever resisted the psychological compulsion to turn away from past unpleasant experiences and to forget or misinterpret them.

If she had remained a pure intellectual, Simone Weil's affinity with the greatest Jewish philosopher of modern Europe, Spinoza, would be even more obvious than it is. In one of her most difficult essays—in the book published after her death under the title *Intuitions pré-chrétiennes*—there is a passage which forms a pendant to the passage quoted on page 72, where she claims that the mystics are the only legitimate users of the language of love. In this essay, a discussion of mathematics leads her to the conclusion that mathematical thought is the essential scientific thought and that, contrary to what is often said, mathematics is a science of nature, and indeed the only one—the other sciences being simply particular applications of mathematics.

> man experiences necessity both as an obstacle and as a condition for making his will effective; consequently, this effort is always slightly falsified by the illusions which are irreducibly associated with the exercise of will. To conceive necessity purely and without illusion, it must be separated from its material framework and thought of as a web of interrelated and interdependent conditions. This pure and conditioned necessity is nothing other than the subject of mathematics.[2]

In other words, the force to which everything in the world is subject is itself obedient to this necessity; but the mathematician cannot conceive it perfectly unless he is able to liberate a part of his mind from subjection to force—and this is an effort similar to religious contemplation, because it means that a part of his mind becomes detached from material needs. "If one succeeds in doing this, one is able to understand the play of forces in accordance with which the satisfaction of needs is granted or refused." [3] Seen in this way, mathematics is hardly distinguishable from the *amor intellectualis dei*. The essay in which this passage occurs is one of those which Simone Weil would almost certainly have revised and rearranged before publication. It fills more than 160 pages and forms part of the work she did in Marseilles in 1941–42 with a view to collaboration with Father Perrin in a collection of texts illustrating Christian truth in non-Christian and pre-Christian thought. It includes comments on the Homeric hymn to Demeter and the Scottish ballad, "The Duke o'Norroway," and some long commentaries on Sophocles, Aeschylus, Plato, Philolaus, and the Pythagoreans. One is continually reminded of Spinoza by the reasoning with which she relates these themes to the doctrines of Christianity, especially the Gospel of St John, and to the principles of mathematics. But the essay is a quarry of ideas rather than a finished building. As an example of its style, here are some rather formidably rational reflexions upon the comfort to be derived in misfortune from an understanding of its inevitability.

> The necessary connexions, which constitute the very reality of the world, have themselves no reality except as the object of the act of intellectual attention. This correlation between necessity and the free act of attention is a marvel. And the greater the indispensable effort of attention, the plainer the marvel becomes. It is much more obvious as regards the fundamental truths concerning what are called irrational numbers, like the square root of two, than as regards the fundamental

truths concerning integers. To conceive the former with the same rigour as the latter, to conceive them as rigorously necessary, calls for a much greater effort of attention. Therefore they are much more precious. . . . We confer, so far as it lies in us, the plenitude of reality upon the objects and creatures around us when we add to intellectual attention that even higher attention which is acceptance, consent, love. But the very fact that the relations which compose the texture of necessity are dependent upon the act performed by our attention makes them something which belongs to us and which we can love. Thus, every human being who suffers will find some relief, if he has ever so little elevation of mind, when he conceives clearly the necessary connexion of causes and effects which produces his suffering.[4]

The other essay in *Intuitions pré-chrétiennes* is a historical sketch of Greek science, which contains a number of ideas upon which a nonmathematician like the present writer cannot comment. To give one example—she refers to the fact that Book Five of Euclid, whose content is attributed to Eudoxus, the friend of Plato and pupil of Archytas, contains the theory of the real numbers, which was rediscovered by modern mathematicians within the last hundred years, in ignorance of the fact that it already existed in a perfect form in Euclid. Her comment is that "after the destruction of Greek civilisation the theory was lost, although Euclid still survived, simply because people were no longer able to understand the state of mind to which it corresponded."

Simone Weil's last book, *The Need for Roots*, in contrast with *Intuitions pré-chrétiennes*, appears to be approximately in the form in which she might have published it. As it stands, it is certainly the most complete statement of her position, because it synthesises her political and social ideas with the religious preoccupation which claimed so much of her thought from 1938 onwards. The book is divided into three parts, of which the first consists of some general considerations on the nature of rights and duties and of the physical and spiritual needs of human beings. In the second part she identifies the need which is the least understood and the most flagrantly unfulfilled in modern society and describes it by making use of a concept (*l'enracinement*) which is difficult to define in French and even more so in English because we have no satisfactory word for it. 'Rootedness' and 'uprootedness' are fairly accurate, though clumsy, translations of *enracinement* and *déracinement*, but they do not cover such a wide range of meaning. For example, Simone Weil identifies *le déracinement*—uprootedness or deracination—as the almost universal malady of our age and also as the essence of the proletarian condition. A proletariat is a class of people without roots in their own country, who live in it like immigrants. The need to be rooted in one's environment and, still more, in one's cultural and historical past, is as essential for the soul as roots in the soil are for a plant. Simone Weil maintains that not only the nineteenth century urban working class and not only all twentieth-century Americans of all classes, but also the whole of Western society and all those countries, like Japan, where western industrialism is widely established, have been or are becoming proletarianised, in the sense that their way of life has spiritually uprooted them.

In the second part of the book, having described the effect of uprootedness in France, first upon the industrial worker and then upon the rural worker, she presents the modern Nation-State as the symbol and product of a civilisation without roots. The feeling of patriotism, which the State tries to monopolise, is nothing new in the world; but it has been directed in the past to a wide range of collectivities, from the village or group of villages, and the region or province, to much larger groups such as Christendom or Islam, or a group of nations or parts of nations. (She instances Britanny, Ireland, Wales and Cornwall as regions which might, though today they do not, feel themselves to represent, on a certain level, a cultural community.) Today, by what she calls a geographical deracination, all these bonds of attachment, and even the collectivities which inspired them, have practically disappeared and nothing remains but the nation, or rather the State—because it is impossible to define a nation except as the aggregate of territories administered by a single State machine. "One could say that in our day all other bonds of attachment have been replaced by money and the State." [5]

Having morally assassinated everything which was, territorially speaking, smaller than itself, the State has turned its own territorial frontiers into prison walls for thought. To anyone who reads history, it is staggering to discover how much vital and fertile exchange of thought there was in the Middle Ages, or in pre-Roman antiquity, over vast geographical areas, in spite of the fact that all our modern improved methods of communication were lacking. Whereas today, although frontiers are not yet impassable (at least between countries outside the Iron Curtain) "all contact with foreign ways of thinking, in every sphere, demands a mental effort in order to get across the frontier. The effort required is considerable, and quite a number of people are not prepared to make it. Even in the case of those who do, the fact that such an effort has to be made prevents the formation of organic links across the frontiers." [6]

So there is nothing narrow or reactionary in Simone

Weil's emphasis on the need for strengthening our roots in the past. As the preceding passage shows, it is the aim of her attack on the State to aerate, refresh, and enlarge the human environment; and she would do this by reviving loyalty to other environments, both larger and smaller than the State. She would have a Breton or Provençal be equally loyal to Europe, to France, and to Britanny or Provence; and she would modify or restrict the functions of the Nation-State in order to give effective reality to the larger and smaller units.

The third part of *The Need for Roots* begins with a survey of the methods available to the Free French in London for rallying and inspiring the Resistance in France. De Gaulle's group, being based entirely on free consent and having no authority over the French people, has a purely symbolic position which is exactly as it should be, she says, for making known to the world the voice of France, "a voice whose authority is not based on physical power, which was destroyed by the defeat, nor on glory, which was wiped out in shame; but first on an elevation of thought which matches the present tragedy, and secondly, on a spiritual tradition which is engraved on the hearts of all peoples." [7]

This has an inspirational note, but Simone Weil was never carried away by her own eloquence and, as is clear in her letter from New York to Jean Wahl she was quick to detect and denounce the symptoms of group self-righteousness. In the preceding section of the book she has a lot to say about the danger of deifying one's own nation and she reminds her Resistance colleagues that "there was once a nation which believed itself to be holy" and things turned out very badly for it. "It is strange indeed to reflect," she adds, "the the Pharisees were the resisters in that nation and the publicans the collaborators, and then to remind oneself what were Christ's relations with each of these two national groups." [8] But her astringent intellectual detachment certainly did not weaken her own support for the French Resistance.

From the problem of how to reach the minds and hearts of the French in German-occupied France the transition is easy to the postwar problem of how to revive civilisation by strengthening the few fragile roots which are all that remain from our past inheritance; and in the third part of the book she identifies four main obstacles which will make the task impossible unless they are removed. They are: our false sense of greatness, our degraded sense of justice, our idolisation of money, and our lack of religious inspiration. In discussing these problems she reveals her quintessential thought, developed to a point of maturity astonishing in a woman of only thirty-four; but since the discussion forms an integral part of the book as a whole it will be best approached through a more detailed examination of the two preceding parts.

She begins by explaining why the subject of the book is obligations and not rights. "It is meaningless to say that men have, on the one hand, rights and, on the other hand, duties. . . . A man, taken by himself, has only duties, among which are certain duties towards himself." [9] Rights are merely obligations seen from a particular point of view; a right is not effectual in itself but only in relation to the obligation to which it corresponds, in so far as that obligation is recognised. An obligation which goes unrecognised loses none of the full force of its existence, whereas a right which nobody recognises is nothing much. "A man left alone in the universe would have no rights whatever, but he would have obligations." [10] Unlike rights, therefore, obligations are independent of conditions. Like beauty and like justice, they belong to a realm outside this world.

But the men of 1789, not recognising any such realm, made the disastrous blunder of emphasising rights, which are relative, instead of obligations, which are absolute, and since, at the same time, they wanted to lay down absolute principles, they created a linguistic and intellectual confusion which has contributed largely to the social and political confusion of the present day.

Basically, according to Simone Weil, there is, "in the realm of human affairs," only one eternal obligation—towards the human being as such. This obligation is unconditional and, so far as this world is concerned, it has no foundation. "If it is founded on something, that something, whatever it is, does not form part of our world." [11] Its only verification in this world is the common consent accorded by the universal conscience. "It finds expression in some of the oldest written texts which have come down to us. It is recognised by everybody without exception in every single case where it is not opposed by interest or passion. And it is in relation to it that we measure our progress." [12]

From this point, by a concise but rather difficult transition, we proceed to some concrete examples of how the obligation is fulfilled. A direct and eternal obligation—so the argument appears to run—is owed only towards the human being as such, and not towards any collectivity, because collectivities have no eternal destiny. But the fact that a human being possesses an eternal destiny imposes only one obligation: respect.

The obligation is only fulfilled if the respect is effectively expressed in a real, not a fictitious way; and this can only be done, through the medium of men's earthly needs.[13]

The most obvious obligation, therefore, and the model for all the others, is to feed the hungry.

> To no matter whom the question may be put in general terms, nobody thinks a man is innocent if, possessing food in abundance, he finds someone dying of hunger on his doorstep and passes by without giving him anything.[14]

With Simone Weil any piece of reasoning, however abstract, is always closely related to something concrete and simple like giving a man a piece of bread.

The soul has needs which, according to Simone Weil, are as material and earthly as those of the body; and their nonsatisfaction leaves the soul in a state analogous to that of a starved or multilated body. Both in her "profession of faith" and in *The Need for Roots* these needs of the soul are listed and the list is an original one, equally in content and in the way it is compiled. To the shocked surprise of some readers it contains such items as obedience, punishment, hierarchy and "disciplined participation in a common task of public value." But Simone Weil, more realistically than her critics, conceives most of the soul's needs in complementary couples; thus recognising the contradictions which are always the terminus of human thought if it is pushed far enough "in this world." She therefore couples the "disciplined participation in a common task of public value" with "personal initiative within this participation" and in the same way hierarchy is coupled with equality, punishment with honour, and security with risk. ("The fear of violence or of hunger or of any other extreme evil is a sickness of the soul. The boredom produced by a complete absence of risk is also a sickness of the soul.") And as for obedience, she has the courage to point out that "there are any number of signs showing that the men of our age have now for a long time been starved of obedience. But advantage has been taken of the fact to give them slavery." [15]

Obedience, in the list of the soul's needs, is coupled with liberty and is qualified by the adjective "consented." It is defined as "what one concedes to an authority because one judges it to be legitimate." Consented obedience, she adds, is not possible towards a political power established by conquest or *coup d'état*, nor towards an economic power based on money. Thus the human soul is starved of obedience in any society in which the principal motive is desire for gain, because the essence of obedience is consent and consent is not a thing that can be bought and sold. Further, since anybody who is starved of obedience is ill in his soul, any society which is governed by a sovereign leader who is answerable to nobody is in the hands of a sick man.

It is a difficult problem to reconcile obedience with liberty, but it is even more so, perhaps, to reconcile equality with hierarchy (which she defines as "the scale of responsibilities"). If she does not solve the problem, she at least makes a realistic approach. She knows that in fact equality and inequality must somehow be combined. This involves, for example, imposing on each man "burdens corresponding to the power and well-being he enjoys, and corresponding risks in cases of incapacity or neglect." But once again money is the stumbling block. It is not differences in kind but differences in degree that are felt as inequality, so the purely quantitative differences established by money introduce the feeling of inequality everywhere. From this point of view, she says, the French Revolution merely substituted for the stable inequality of the *ancien régime* a fluid inequality of competition for wealth. The one form of inequality is as unwholesome as the other.

In discussing freedom of expression as a need of the soul, Simone Weil sharply dissociates it from what is usually mentioned with it, freedom of association. Apart from natural groups, such as the family, association is not a need of the soul but merely an expedient in the practical affairs of life. "What has been called freedom of association up to now has been in fact freedom for associations. But associations have not got to be free; they are instruments and should be subservient." [16] On the other hand, "complete, unlimited freedom of expression for every sort of opinion, without the least restriction or reserve, is an absolute need of the intelligence. Consequently it is a need of the soul, for when the intelligence is ill at lease the whole soul is sick." [17]

She goes so far as to suggest that certain publications might be authorised in which writers, without being held to commit themselves or to be offering advice to their readers, could set forth the arguments in favour of every conceivable bad cause.

> It would be publicly recognised that the object of such works was not to define their authors' attitudes in face of the problems of life, but to contribute, by preliminary researches, towards a complete and correct tabulation of data concerning each problem. The law would see to it that their publication did not involve any risk of any kind for the author.[18]

Outside these special publications, however, she would not allow an author to shelter behind the doctrine of art for art's sake if his writings were found to have a demoralising effect. (Supposing, to quote the example she gives, some suggestible reader of Gide's *Les Caves du Vatican* should imitate the hero's "gratuitous act" of pushing someone out of a train.) Such an author would be called upon to state publicly whether or not his writings express his personal attitude. "If he is not prepared to do so, it is simple enough to punish him. If he lies, it is simple enough to discredit him." [19]

If these proposals seem impracticable or utopian, her views on political propaganda and journalism will seem even more so. But they would not be unreasonable in any society which had adopted the moral code expounded in her profession of faith, and it is on that assumption that she is writing. On the same assumption, what could be more reasonable than that "publicity should be rigorously controlled by law and its volume very considerably reduced; it should also be severely prohibited from ever dealing with subjects which belong to the domain of thought."? [20]

All problems to do with freedom of expression, she continues, are clarified when we remember that freedom is a need of the intelligence and that intelligence resides solely in the human being as an individual. There is no such thing as collective exercise of the intelligence. "It follows that no group can legitimately claim freedom of expression, because no group has the slightest need of it." People may group themselves together to defend their interests, within limits, but "such associations should not be allowed to have anything to do with ideas."

One of Simone Weil's major themes is her criticism of that spurious self-sacrifice and renunciation which creates group solidarity, when people renounce the first person singular only to substitute for it the first person plural.

In that case the terms in relation are no longer myself and the other, or myself and others, but homogeneous

fragments of "us." . . . According to Philolaus' postu-
late, therefore, they cannot be linked by a harmony; they
are linked by themselves, and without mediation. There
is no distance between them, no empty space into which
God can flow. Nothing is more opposed to friendship
than solidarity, whether it is a solidarity of comradeship,
or of personal sympathy, or of sharing the same social
milieu, the same politics, the same nation, or the same
religious confession. Those thoughts which explicitly or
implicitly involve the first person plural are infinitely
further from justice even than those which involve the
first person singular; because the first person plural
cannot be one of three terms in a mathematical proportion whose middle term is God.[21]

The above passage is part of her analysis, in *Intuitions
pré-chrétiennes*, of the Pythagorean formula "Friendship is an equality composed of harmony." It explains
her proposal in *The Need for Roots* that the expression of opinion by any group should be forbidden by
law. When a group begins having opinions it inevitably tends to impose them on its members, and in the
end they are compelled to leave the group if they
express opinions contrary to its own.

But a break with any group to which one belongs always
involves suffering—at least of a sentimental kind. And
just as danger and the risk of suffering are healthy and
necessary elements in the sphere of action, so they are
unhealthy influences in the exercise of the intelligence.
A fear, even a passing one, always either sways or tautens
the mind, according to the degree of courage, and that is
all that is required to damage the extremely delicate and
fragile instrument of precision which constitutes our
intelligence. Even friendship is, from this point of view,
a great danger. The intelligence is defeated as soon as
the expression of one's thoughts is preceded, explicitly or
implicitly, by the little word "we." And when the light
of the intelligence grows dim, it is not very long before
the love of good becomes lost.[22]

So much, among other things, for the editorial "we."
And as regards journals of opinion (which, if they are
to stimulate thought, and not merely bludgeon
people's minds, ought not to appear more often than
weekly): "Freedom of opinion can be claimed
solely—and even then with reservations—by the journalist, not by the journal; for it is only the journalist
who is capable of forming an opinion." A journal can
be suppressed, therefore, without the slightest infringe-
ment of freedom of opinion, so long as the editorial
staff are left free to go on publishing elsewhere. Finally, there should be a complete prohibition of "all
propaganda of whatever kind by the radio or daily
press. These two instruments would only be allowed to
be used for nontendentious information." [23]

Does all this seem preposterous? If so, it is a measure
of how urgently it needed to be said.

The remainder of the book is concerned with that
"most important and least recognised need of the
soul" which she calls "being rooted" (*l'enracinement*). All the value that can be possessed by any
natural group or collectivity, as such, (the family, the
religious or linguistic or cultural group) consists in the
fact that it nourishes the roots of the soul. To the
extent that it does this, there is an obligation to respect
and defend it, and in some cases even to sacrifice one's
life for it. But this by no means implies the superiority
of the collectivity over the individual. On the contrary,
if and when a collectivity is valuable it is only because
it is food for human souls, and because, unlike material
food, it is unique and irreplaceable. One loaf of bread
can be substituted for another, but each family, each
cultural tradition, is unique.

Because of its continuity in time, the collectivity is

already moving into the future; "it contains food not only for the souls of the living but also for the souls of beings yet unborn." And with its roots in the past it is the sole agency for preserving our most precious inheritance, the spiritual achievements of the dead. "The sole earthly reality which is directly connected with the eternal destiny of man is the irradiating light of those who have known how to become fully conscious of that destiny, transmitted from generation to generation." [24]

Such is the kind of medium in which the soul needs to be rooted; and it needs multiple roots. Every human being "needs to receive almost the whole of his moral, intellectual and spiritual life through the medium of the various environments of which he forms a natural part." [25]

Using this criterion, she examines the state of Western culture, more particularly in France, in the first half of the twentieth century and diagnoses two major causes of deracination. These two causes are: money and modern education. If the Greek tradition, in which all studies are related to religious contemplation, had not been soon abandoned after its brief revival at the Renaissance, then the splitting up of education into separate unrelated subjects could not have occurred. But what in fact did happen was that culture developed within a restricted medium, divorced from everyday life, largely influenced by technical science, and subdivided into unrelated specialisms. The result is that each subject is regarded as an end in itself ("deracination breeds idolatry"); and we have a culture out of contact with the common life of this world and without a window opening on to any other.

> Nowadays a man can belong to so-called cultured circles without, on the one hand, having any sort of conception about human destiny or, on the other hand, being

aware, for example, that all the constellations are not visible at all seasons of the year.[26]

If it is difficult to impart this culture to the workers, says Simone Weil, it is not because it is too high for them but because it is too low. And its only effect, whether they try to enter into it or whether it remains an alien country to them, is to increase their sense of uprootedness. Culture, as we know it today, is no more than "an instrument manipulated by teachers for manufacturing more teachers, who, in their turn will manufacture still more teachers." [27]

The latter part of *The Need for Roots* is concerned with the state of religion and science in the modern world, and my next two chapters will be an attempt to pick out the main thread of the argument. Since the book itself is extremely condensed and closely reasoned, it is impossible to do justice to it in a *précis*. But it contains most of the essence of Simone Weil's thought, and if my *précis* of it reads so provocatively as to drive the reader to consult the book itself, he will certainly have no cause to regret the provocation.

SINCE SIMONE WEIL'S DEATH the process of deracination has accelerated, perhaps even more rapidly than she foresaw. In 1943, as we saw in chapter five, she was still able to think of the African peoples as the responsibility of Europe as a whole and to hope that they might be helped towards "a happy village life." It would be folly, she wrote, "even in those cases where it would be practicable, to say nothing of those where it would not," [1] to turn them into nations on the European model, whether democratic or otherwise. "There are all too many nations in the world already." And as regards Europe, while present trends continue there is no more than an academic interest in her plan for decentralising industry or in her ideas for reviving rural life by ceremonies linking the cycle of the agricultural year with the Gospel parables of sowing, reaping, and viticulture. Her idea was that people should be educated in such a way that a man's job should be for him "a window open on the world." But the television screen and the window of the touring Pullman have since taken care of that; and as for education, it now means only two things: on the one hand, technical instruction, and on the other hand, keeping up with the Joneses by cultivating your personality and learning how to make what is pleasantly called "creative" use of your leisure. So we need not linger over her two chapters on the deracinated factory worker and the deracinated peasant. We will only note that even if the day comes when all unskilled work is performed by "mechanical slaves" and when only a small minority wish, or are required, to become skilled workers, people will still need to find *something* to do in addition to viewing and touring. And the more deracinated they are, the more difficult it will be for them to find anything worth doing.

The world which Simone Weil thought a man's job should reveal to him was a world which can be a stepping-stone towards another world; and as we know from her profession of faith, she conceived the act of passing over as an act of attention. The inspiration for this act comes largely from the "irradiating light" of those who have achieved it in the past; but deracination destroys our links with the past.

How this evil can be remedied is the theme of the third part of *The Need for Roots*, but before we come to it there is a word to be said about her view of the modern State as an agent of "geographical deracination." For the French in London in 1943 a clear conception of the meaning of patriotism—that is to say, of patriotism as a virtue in contradistinction to the idolatry of the State which is what the word stands for today—was peculiarly important, and Simone Weil correctly observes that it is a subject which has scarcely ever received any serious study. As a contribution towards it she offers a brief historical sketch:

> The nation is a recent innovation. In the Middle Ages allegiance was owed to the lord, or the city, or both, and by extension to territorial areas not very clearly defined. The sentiment we call patriotism certainly existed, often to a very intense degree; but its object was territorially indefinite.[2]

The area of country to which patriotism extended was variable according to circumstances. It was only in recent times, she continues, that a definite, circumscribed thing was permanently installed as an object of patriotic devotion. Until then, patriotism had been something diffuse and versatile, which could expand or contract according to degrees of affinity or common danger.

> It was mixed up with different kinds of loyalty—loyalty to other men, a lord, a king, or a city. The whole formed something very confused, but also very human. To express the sense of obligation every one feels towards his country, people would usually talk about "the public" or "the public good," an expression which can serve equally well to indicate a village, town, province, France, Christendom or Mankind.[3]

She then outlines the development of national consciousness in France up to 1789 and shows that the Revolution revealed three totally different conceptions of patriotism. First, the spirit of the Revolution, which, for a year or two, was both French and international; it consisted of pride in the French people's illusory achievement of sovereignty and a generous ambition to assist all peoples towards the same achievement. Second, the spirit of the *ancien régime*, which was a personal and dynastic fidelity to the king. And third, the patriotism of Talleyrand and those like him. These men were in fact the only patriots, according to the sense in which the word is used today, although they were denounced, both by their contemporaries and by posterity, as archtraitors. Accused of serving every regime in turn, what they in fact did was to serve France behind every regime. "But for such men France was neither the sovereign people nor the king; it was the French State. Subsequent events have shown how right they were."[4]

Because, when once the illusion of the sovereign people had been seen manifestly to be an illusion, it could no longer serve as an object of patriotism. And as for royalty, it was like a felled tree which one does not replant. So patriotism was obliged to follow Talleyrand and turn towards the State.

> But thereby it ceased to be popular. For the State was not something brought into being in 1789; it dated from the beginning of the seventeenth century, and shared some of the hatred nursed by the people against the monarchy. Thus it happened that by a political paradox which at first sight seems surprising, patriotism changed to a different social class and political camp. It had been on the Left; it went over to the Right.[5]

Nevertheless, as was proved in 1914, patriotism did not altogether die out among the French people—and for a very simple reason. Men need something to be loyal to, and in France, as in most modern countries, there was nothing left but the State. It need not necessarily be one's own State. For many Leftist intellectuals and for a section of the working class in Europe between the wars the Russian State was the focus of patriotism. And it is true of course that the Church still exists. But religion has abdicated. What our vaunted religious "tolerance" in fact amounts to is that man's relationship to God, so far from being too sacred a matter for any external authority to interfere in, is of so little importance that the State can safely leave it to each man's particular fancy. Simone Weil quotes a revealing French commonplace, which is equally familiar in other countries and which can be adapted as follows: "Whether Catholics, Protestants, Jews or Free Thinkers, we're all Americans," as though one should say "Whether from the East, the West or the Middle West, we're all Americans"—thus equating one's religion with an arbitrary subdivision of a larger area. And the Church itself adopts the same attitude. Simone Weil quotes an official pronouncement which begins: "Not only from the Christian point of view, but, more generally, from the human point of view." "As though," she comments, "the Christian point of view—which either has no meaning at all, or else claims to encompass everything in this world and the next—possessed a smaller degree of generality than the human point of view. It is impossible to conceive a more terrible admission of religious bankruptcy." [6]

We have already seen that Simone Weil's conception of a Christianity which "encompasses everything" differed from the orthodox conception, which is verbally similar, of "catholicity"; and we have also seen that the difference is sometimes obscured by her way of expressing herself. In the same way her criticism of what is called religious tolerance may be misunderstood if one forgets that the kind of tolerance she is referring to is in fact a kind of indifference. Real tolerance, as she understood it, means active sympathy and encouragement for anything that can be what she called a "vital medium" for the soul, any tradition or any group or any social environment in which the soul can find roots that will give it spiritual food. One of these media is the nation or country to which one belongs; but it is only one among others, some larger and some smaller, which are equally necessary to us; and since one's country must be full of imperfections, like every other human collectivity, to worship it in the spirit of "my country, right or wrong" is to commit the sin of idolatry. What the world requires, she says, is a new form of patriotism, and for this it is essential to disentangle the idea of one's country from that of the cold, aggressive, exclusive, monopolistic mechanism called the State. The thought of one's country can inspire pity and charity.

> This poignantly tender feeling for some beautiful, precious, fragile and perishable object has a warmth about it which the sentiment of national grandeur altogether lacks. . . . Isn't a man easily capable of acts of heroism to protect his children, or his aged parents? And yet there is no prestige of grandeur attached to them. A perfectly pure love for one's country has a kinship with the feelings which his young children, his aged parents, or a beloved wife inspire in a man.[7]

Such feelings are totally unlike those connected with the State, which always suggests ideas of glory and grandeur and aggressiveness. Whereas:

> The compassion felt for fragility is always associated with love for real beauty, because we are keenly conscious of the fact that the existence of the really beautiful things ought to be assured for ever, and is not.
>
> One can love France either for the glory which would seem to ensure for her a prolonged existence in time and space; or else one can love her as something which, being earthly, can be destroyed, and is all the more precious on that account.
>
> These are two distinct ways of loving. . . . But the second alone is legitimate for a Christian because it alone is in keeping with Christian humility.[8]

The eighty pages of the second part of *The Need for Roots* give an incomparable historical and political sketch of the relations between the individual and the State in France right up to the Second World War. They ought to be required reading not only for students of modern France but for all politicians and sociologists, because they are relevant to the same problem in all modern countries: the State as a collective animal, the mass ego summing up all the individual egoisms of its members; the State as an idol, demanding holocausts of its citizens; the State as a chronic invalid, secretly hated by his family because their sacrifices for him exceed their love for him; the State as a governess to be hoodwinked; the State as a shop to be plundered or cheated, and so on. A love-hate relationship culminating in the emergence of the Leader, in whom the cold, metallic features of the state, which are so difficult to love, are disguised under the appearance of a man of flesh and blood. This latter phenomenon, she predicts, writing in 1943, is not likely soon to decline and may well have some unpleasant surprises in store for us, "because the art, so well understood in Hollywood, of manufacturing stars out of any sort of human material gives any sort of person the opportunity of presenting himself for the adoration of the masses." [9] Did she forsee that twenty years after her death political journalism would be dominated by the word "image"?

But valuable though they are in themselves, her observations on French history and politics must take a subsidiary place in any short sketch of her work as a whole. Her desire to cure French patriotism of its fixation upon false grandeur leads to a larger problem which is the main theme of *The Need for Roots*. This theme is, of course, the strengthening of the few fragile roots which are all that western civilisation still possesses, and which contain the only hope of its revival; and this, for her, involves attacking the four major problems mentioned in the last chaper: our false sense of greatness, our degraded sense of justice, our idolisation of money, and our lack of religious inspiration.

Our conception of greatness is the very one which has inspired Hitler's whole life. When we denounce his conception, without the faintest suspicion that it is also ours, the angels must either weep or laugh, if there happen to be angels who interest themselves in our propaganda.[10]

Quoted in isolation, this statement looks very provocative. Some readers may find it hardly less so in its context in the book; and they may be equally provoked by some of the historical arguments adduced in its support. Men worship force, says Simone Weil, and they always have done so. Even pity goes only to the strong, and not to the weak. The affliction of the weak is either not noticed at all or else is an object of repulsion. It is true that the defeated can inspire pity, and even sentimentality, but only if their defeat is provisional and the possibility of revenge is not ruled out. For things that have been utterly destroyed, no compassion is felt. Who feels any today, she asks, for Jericho, Gaza, Tyre, Sidon, Carthage, Numantia, or Peru before the time of Columbus? And if it is objected that all that was long ago, then why, asks Simone Weil, are so many more people concerned nowadays about the interests of factory workers than of peasants? (Writing in 1965, she might perhaps have contrasted the amount of concern felt for Negroes with the amount felt for Tibetans.)

History, she maintains, is a series of accounts of successful crime, written by the criminals. But her criticism of the modern conception of greatness does not rely solely upon the historical argument, which some may find tendentious. It is also perfectly consistent with the deterministic psychology outlined on page 96 above: that man is subject in his entire being, mental as well as physical, to a blind force completely indifferent to the good, and that what men call justice is usually no more than an index of the relation of forces at any given moment.

To correct our standards, we must learn to pay attention to the extremely rare examples of true justice which history affords. One of them is the *Iliad*, in which the truth about force is courageously and bitterly acknowledged, but not condoned. Unlike almost all other successful criminals, the Greeks did not calumniate their victims. Instead, they wrote the greatest epic of the West as a testimony in their favour. Not only is the poem so impartial that one would hardly guess the poet was Greek and not Trojan, but it makes clear, so Simone Weil maintains, that of the two sides it was Troy and not Greece that repre- sented civilisation.

As for the Romans: "If I am not mistaken," she writes, "among all the facts concerning the Romans which we find in ancient history, there is only one example of a perfectly pure act of goodness." At the time of the proscriptions under the triumvirate a certain Roman slaveowner, whose name was on the list for execution, was hidden by his slaves, who loved him. When soldiers came to make a search the slaves refused to betray their master, and, although tortured, they persisted in their refusal. But from his hiding place the master was able to see the tortures and was unable to bear it. He came out and gave himself up to the soldiers, who immediately killed him.

> Whoever has his heart in the right place, if he had to choose between several destinies, would choose to be either that master or one of those slaves, rather than one of the Scipios, or Caesar, or Cicero, or Augustus, or Virgil, or even one of the Gracchi.[11]

She gives a third example, this time from mediaeval history. Louis IX of France is reported to have said that for a layman the correct method of controversy, if anyone uttered doubts or heresies in his presence, was to slay him. Yet Louis IX was canonised. And why not? people will ask. His idea of theological contro-

versy may have been brutal, but it was in the spirit of
his age, which, being seven centuries earlier than our
own, was proportionately unenlightened. But this is a
lie, says Simone Weil. Morality is the same in all ages;
and one proof of this was given by the Catholics
of Béziers, a few years before the time of St. Louis.
They suffered themselves to be exterminated rather
than hand over to the Inquisition their heretical Albigensian fellow citizens. "The Church has forgotten to
place them in the ranks of her martyrs, a distinction
which she accords to inquisitors killed by their po-
tential victims. Nor have the amateurs of tolerance,
enlightenment, and the lay spirit during the past three
centuries done anything to commemorate this event.
Such a heroic form of the virtue they so insipidly label
tolerance they would have found disconcerting." [12]

It is absolutely false, says Simone Weil, to imagine
that there is some providential mechanism by which
what is best in any given period is transmitted to the
memory of posterity. On the contrary, by the very
nature of things, it is false greatness which is transmitted—though there is transmitted along with it a
tiny quantity of genuine greatness. If is for us to learn
to distinguish it, but "the spirit of truth, justice and
love has nothing whatever to do with questions of
date; it is eternal; . . . an act of cruelty in the tenth
century is exactly as cruel, neither more nor less so,
than an act of cruelty in the nineteenth." She does,
however, admit, at least in theory, that one must use
some historical imagination.

In identifying an act of cruelty, it is necessary to bear in
mind the circumstances, the different meanings attached to acts and words, the symbolic language peculiar
to each environment; but once an act has been indubi-

tably recognised as being cruel, it is a horrible one, whenever and wherever it happens to have been committed.[13]

This would allow a certain latitude in judging the behaviour of people like St. Louis, which Simone Weil does not always seem to avail herself of.

But what is more important in her interpretation of history is her insistence that the notion of moral progress is pure superstition. In general, she says, the whole progressive myth, "the poison of our age," [14] is a product of the alliance of early Christianity with imperial Rome, when it became the official Roman religion. It makes the Redemption a temporal instead of an eternal operation and is based on the idea of a divine system of education, preparing men so as to make them fit to receive Christ's message, and upon the obliteration of the spiritual values, "perfectly continuous with Christianity," [15] which already existed in the countries destroyed by Rome.

> This fitted in with the hopes of a universal conversion of the nations and the end of the world, regarded as both being imminent. But when neither of these two things took place, at the end of sixteen or seventeen centuries, this notion of progress was prolonged beyond the temporal context of the Christian revelation. Consequently, it was bound to turn against Christianity.
>
> In Revelation there is no trace of this idea. Is there any in St. Paul? It doesn't seem to me so.[16]

So the progressive myth, originally Christian, was turned into a lay dogma. And since it teaches that an act which would be considered inhuman today may have been great and good in the past, "it dishonours goodness by making it an affair of fashion." [17]

What, she asks, is to prevent a modern youth from reading history and saying to himself: "I feel in my bones that the time when humanity was a virtue is now

over, and that we are returning to an age of inhumanity"? What is to prevent him from imagining a
cyclical succession instead of a straight line?

But the admiration for spurious greatness is not
confined to our interpretation of history. In literature
and the other arts what is called greatness is very often
the product of talent, and not of genius. "There is a
certain domination of literary talent over the centuries
which corresponds to the domination of political
talent in space." [18] This domination is "equally temporal, equally attached to the realm of matter and force,
equally base"; [19] and it is an object for sale and
exchange in open market. Poets like Ariosto, and
Virgil too, made in effect a sort of commercial bargain
with their patrons—which was openly expressed by
Ariosto, though Virgil was too discreet: Give me your
favour and money, and I will make you illustrious. But
poetry is not something for sale, and writers of this
kind, however great their talent, should be described
by some other name than poet.

Talent, as everybody knows, has nothing to do with
morality, and yet not only in history but in all studies,
the humanities and science alike, it is talent that is
held up for the student's admiration. The conclusion
naturally drawn by the student is that virtue is the
badge of mediocrity. Indeed, the very word virtue has
by now come to sound slightly ridiculous.

At this point Simone Weil introduces an idea which
seems to me an essential clue to all her work. If it is
true, then all her other ideas fall into place and her
scattered essays and notes on all the multifarious
subjects that occupied her can be seen to form parts of
a coherent whole—and not only coherent but also
essentially harmonious in spite of the unevenness and

personal idiosyncrasy which are inseparable from any original human endeavour. If it is untrue, then her work is no more than a quarry of ideas from which a reader may pick and choose according to his fancy. This is her statement of it:

> It is true that talent has no connexion with morality; but, also, there is no greatness in talent. It is untrue that there is no connexion between perfect beauty, perfect truth, perfect justice. They are far more than just connected; they form a single mysterious unity, for the good is one.[20]

The proposition that the good is one may seem excessively abstract, even to a serious reader—quite apart from the sort of reader who will pretend not to understand the meaning of words like "good" and "is" and "one." But it is simply monotheism; it means that there is only one God. Polytheism, says Simone Weil, does not mean "indulging in fancies about Apollo and Diana,"[21] it means believing that, instead of one good, there are a number of separate and mutually independent goods, each of which can be pursued for its own sake; art for art's sake, truth for truth's sake, morality for morality's sake, and so on. As against this, she asserts the truth of monotheism. And if this still seems too abstract, her very next paragraph makes it sufficiently concrete, at least so far as art is concerned.

> There exists a focal point of greatness where the genius which creates beauty, and the genius which reveals truth, and heroism, and sanctity are indistinguishable. Already, as one approaches this point, one can see the different forms of greatness tending to merge into one another. In Giotto, it is not possible to distinguish between the genius of the painter and the Franciscan spirit; nor in the pictures and poems produced by the Zen sect in China between the painter's or poet's genius and the state of mystical illumination. . . . From the

purely poetic point of view, without taking into account
anything else, it is infinitely preferable to have written
the Canticle of St Francis of Assisi, that jewel of perfect
beauty, rather than the entire works of Victor Hugo.[22]

Parenthetically—if Simone Weil ever read the Abbé
Bremond's book on prayer and poetry, she must have
been shocked by its conclusion that, while poetry is
only less exalted than prayer, the poets themselves are
a "curious lot" and "not to be taken too tragically,"
and even more shocked by the Abbé's approval of
some remarks of Coventry Patmore which he para-
phrases in these extraordinary words: "Poets are a kind
of half-saints, with the most delicate spiritual insight
and the most unheroic conscience. Their genius seems
to confer on them a sanctity independent of all virtue,
so they can prophesy at their ease, without thereby
incurring any responsibility." [23] A curious lot, indeed!
And yet Bremond's book is partly based on the work of
Middleton Murry, whose ideas about both mysticism
and poetry are very close to Simone Weil's.

In addition to Giotto and the Zen artists and St.
Francis, Simone Weil gives, in the passage from which
I have quoted, a number of other examples of artistic
genius approximating to sanctity: Aeschylus, Sophocles, Monteverdi, Velasquez, Bach, Mozart, the *Iliad*,
King Lear, *Phèdre* (but not the rest of Racine), and
the spirit of Romanesque architecture and Gregorian
chant. It is always dangerous to make lists of this kind,
interesting though they are, because they are likely to
sidetrack a discussion. If Velasquez, why not Rem-
brandt? Or Van Gogh? And so on. However, such
quibbles would be ridiculous in this case, because the
list is obviously only a thumbnail illustration of an
idea. But Simone Weil does sometimes make lists
which might fairly be called controversial. In her essay
on Hitler and Rome she makes a list of French writers

between 1400 and 1700 who were "neither servants nor worshippers of force," [24] and in *The Need for Roots* she names only seventeen writers in the whole of French literature in whom the genius of France can be seen in its purity.[25] They are interesting lists, both by their inclusions and their exclusions. Pascal appears only in the first; Bossuet in neither. But as regards the second list, she herself only claims that it may be "fairly accurate"; and in any case the desire to criticise or amend such a list implies that one takes seriously the idea it is meant to illustrate—which, and not the accuracy of the list, is the important point.

To reject the idea amounts to believing that figs can be gathered from thistles. To believe that true greatness in any sphere whatsoever, whether in art or science, or in public or private life, can be the product of anything except goodness is to disbelieve Christ's saying that: "A good tree bringeth forth good fruit, but a corrupt tree bringeth forth evil fruit." True greatness, says Simone Weil, is the good fruit which grows on the good tree, "and the good tree is a disposition of the soul akin to saintliness." [26] The other forms of so-called greatness—which, for her, range from Virgil and Corneille to Napoleon and Hitler—must be distinguished from the genuinely great and then examined dispassionately "like natural curiosities." [27] In practice, in individual cases, she admits that it is possible to make wrong judgements, to mistake false greatness for real and vice versa; but it is vital to maintain the principle of the distinction between the two.

So much for false greatness in history and in art. But the same false values are also found in science and religion. Science will be the subject of the next chapter, but we cannot conclude this one without

reference to an interesting passage on the false religion
of "God for God's sake."

"Never in this world," says Simone Weil, "can there
be any dimensional equality between an obligation
and its object." An obligation is infinite; the object of
it, being something in this world, is not. This is one of
the basic contradictions inherent in the human condition. Like all such contradictions, it cannot be resolved
but can only be recognised, accepted, and used as a
taking off place to rise above the human. In one form
or another, this contradiction weighs upon the lives of
all men at all times (for example, the obligation to
defend one's country). There are various ways of
trying to resolve the contradiction, but all of them are
false. One way is to pretend that there do exist in this
world one or more objects (e.g. a nation, an institu-
tion, a person, a tradition, an art) in which there
inheres an absolute value, an infinity, a perfection,
corresponding to the absoluteness of the obligation.
But to attribute such a value to anything whatsoever in
this world is idolatry. Another way of trying to resolve
the contradiction is to deny all obligations; but although a man can pretend to do this it is in fact
impossible. It amounts to spiritual suicide. "And man
is so made that in him spiritual death is accompanied
by psychological diseases which are in themselves
fatal." So the instinct of self-preservation prevents the
soul from doing more than flirt with the idea of
denying all obligations; and a man who pretends to do
so is almost certainly always lying. "There isn't a man
on earth who doesn't sometimes pronounce an opinion
on good and evil, even if it be only to find fault with
somebody else."

The third way of trying to resolve the contradiction
is the way of false religion. It consists in being prepared
to recognise obligations only towards that which is not

of this world and which can therefore be as absolute
and unlimited as the obligation.

One variety of this particular device is spurious mysticism, spurious contemplation. Another is the practice of
good works carried out in a certain spirit, "for the love of
God," as they say; the unfortunate objects of compassion being nothing but the raw material for the action,
an anonymous means whereby one's love of God can be
manifested. In either case, there is a lie, for "he who
loveth not his brother whom he hath seen, how should
he love God whom he hath not seen?" It is only through
things and individual beings on this earth that human
love can penetrate to what lies beyond.[28]

PROBABLY NOT MANY READERS will know the source of the following quotation:

> Man must never fall into the error of thinking that he is meant to be lord and master of Nature. . . . He will then feel that in a world where planets and suns follow circular trajectories, where moons revolve around planets, where force rules everywhere as sole master over weakness, which it compels to serve it docilely or else destroys, Man cannot live by a separate law of his own.

These words are from Hitler's *Mein Kampf.*[1] Simone Weil quotes them in *The Need for Roots* as a proof that Hitler had reached with perfect accuracy the only possible conclusion that can be drawn from the conception of the world contained in modern science; that is to say, the science which was founded by Galileo, Descartes, and others in the seventeenth century and from which our own is derived.

In other words, Hitler was sufficiently lucid when he wrote that passage to recognise the incompatibility of modern science with humanism. Ever since the eighteenth century, if not earlier, humanists have attempted to believe, first, that force rules supreme over all natural phenomena, and, second, that men can and ought to base their mutual relations upon justice, recognised as such through the application of reason. But how, as Hitler reasonably asks, is it conceivable, if everything in the universe is subject to the rule of force, that man, who is made of flesh and blood and whose mind is at the mercy of sensory impressions, should be exempt from the universal rule?

It was to escape from this dilemma that so many materialist thinkers have resorted to the myth of matter as a machine for manufacturing good. While Marx introduced into matter an imaginary mechanism which unceasingly aspires towards the best, the nineteenth century liberal economists imagined that when force enters the sphere of human relations, in the form of money, it becomes, so long as it is not tampered with by war or politics, an automatic producer of justice. And Hitler, too, says Simone Weil, "after his brief moment of intellectual courage and perspicacity," recoiled from the stark vision of a universe entirely swayed by force, and imagined a mechanism for producing justice.

At this point, by one of her sudden, breathtaking strokes, Simone Weil brings together under the same condemnation Hitler and Aristotle, with a side-glance at Judaism and St. Thomas Aquinas as well. Hitler, she points out, borrowed his justice-producing mechanism from the very people who continually obsessed him by the repulsion which they inspired in him; it was from Judaism that he borrowed the idea of the chosen race, the race destined to become supreme over all and then to establish among its slaves the type of justice suitable to the condition of slavery. And this leads to an attack upon Aristotle, who employed the same mental device for representing force as a generator of justice.

It would be a great mistake to regard these apparent extravagances of Simone Weil as if they were fireworks in the manner of Bernard Shaw. She certainly had no wish to apper audacious or paradoxical, and what are sometimes called her prejudices have always a solid foundation which is anything rather than whimsical or capricious. In this particular case she reasons as follows: Aristotle justified slavery by the argument that, for those who are servile by nature, slavery is the happiest and most just condition; and this is precisely the argument that Hitler required, so as to persuade himself that force, or matter, is a machine for producing good. But a man who draws up an apology for slavery is not a lover of justice. There are thinkers, and St. Thomas among them, who look upon Aristotle as the greatest authority on all subjects of study accessible to human reason, amongst which is justice. To accept as authoritative the ideas of a man who doesn't love justice is an offence against justice; and even though an Aristotelian may reject Aristotle's particular opinion about slavery he inevitably accepts others in which that one was rooted. "Consequently, the existence in contemporary Christianity of a Thomistic current constitutes a bond of complicity—amongst many others, unfortunately—between the Nazis and their opponents." [2]

The resemblance between the Nazis and their opponents (which means all right-thinking people, which means us) is strongly emphasised in *The Need for Roots*. What horrifies us in Hitler is simply our own features, enlarged. But the fact that Hitler was more completely a victim than the average modern man of the false sense of greatness and the false science, which dominate all of us, is in some ways to his credit. He was a pure specimen of the uprooted, half-baked, proletarianised, urban petty bourgeois of the twentieth century. He was fed upon the same lies as the rest of us, the science that knows no law but force and the history that glorifies the triumphs of force. "Who can reproach him," asks Simone Weil, "for putting into practice what he thought he recognised to be the truth? Those who, having in themselves the foundation of the same belief, have not consciously acknowledged it or translated it into act, have only escaped being criminals thanks to the lack of a certain sort of courage which he possessed." [3]

There are only two choices: either to recognize another principle of a different kind at work in the universe, alongside force, or else to accept Hitler's conclusion that force must be the sole ultimate arbiter of human relations also. If we make the first choice, we are in opposition to modern science; if we make the second choice, we are in opposition to humanism. Simone Weil of course makes the first choice. She recognises at work in the universe a totally different principle from that of force—namely, the principle of justice. But she does not fall into the humanist error of imagining that the principle of force gives birth to or manufactures the principle of justice. "Force is not a machine for automatically creating justice. It is a blind mechanism which produces indiscriminately and impartially just or unjust results, but, by the laws of probability, nearly always unjust ones." [4] And the passing of time makes no difference. The infinitesimal proportion of results which happen by chance to be in conformity with justice always remains the same.

Science, therefore, is perfectly correct in what it teaches about the supremacy of force in the world of matter, which includes not only our bodies *but also our minds*; and there is no evolution of justice within that world, as humanists naively suppose. But science, or rather, modern science, is also wrong, because it ignores or excludes from its field of interest the "other reality" which is the source of the principle of justice. Greek science, on the contrary, from which our own is descended, was entirely oriented towards the other reality, and was, indeed, inseparable from religion. It was a form of religious contemplation.

According to Simone Weil's profession of faith, it will be remembered, an orientation towards the other reality is all that is possible for human beings, because that reality is "outside any sphere whatsoever that is accessible to human faculties." She also believed that "all beauty, all truth, all justice, all legitimacy, all order, and all behaviour that is mindful of obligations" have their source in that reality and that they only come into the world through a mind which is oriented towards it. And she believed that the process is governed by a very precise science of "celestial mechanics," whose principles can be studied in the mystical literature of Europe and Asia; in Europe, for example, in the Gospels and in the works of Plato and of St. John of the Cross. Simone Weil's own thoughts on this subject are to be found mainly in *Waiting on God* and *Pensées sans ordre concernant l'amour de Dieu* (especially in the essay on "The Love of God and Affliction," which appears in part in the former and complete in the latter of those two volumes), in the essays on Plato in *Intuitions pré-chrétiennes* and *La Source grecque*, and in her notebooks. This part of her work will be the subject of the next chapter. If one can legitimately make the distinction in a thinker who is so much all of one piece, it represents the more esoteric side of her thought, while *The Need for Roots* represents the more exoteric side.

In the latter book, as we have seen, her subject is the rootlessness of contemporary civilisation, its false science and its lack of religious inspiration, and finally, as always, the problem which continually obsessed her:

the position in society of the manual workers, with
whom she identified herself and whom she thought of
as the anonymous, unprivileged masses. In trying to
outline her ideas today, it is this last point which, at
any rate in Europe and America, most obviously
invites misunderstanding. When she writes about
manual labour, a superficial reader might get the
impression that she thinks the employees in modern
factories are still living in the conditions of the
mid-nineteenth century. And this in spite of the fact
that she had experienced the conditions herself, which
the reader quite possibly never did. However, it is now
thirty years since she worked in the Renault factory in
Paris, and if she were alive today she would no doubt
recognise that even in those thirty years the material
conditions in factories, and to some extent on the land
as well, have become less arduous. But her criticism of
modern America and Europe would not be substan-
tially affected; and, indeed, she would find that the
drift towards proletarianisation had become more, and
not less, pronounced. Modern States tend more and
more to turn their comparatively comfortable subjects
into anonymous masses, and the struggle to emerge
from the mass and acquire 'status' (a euphemism for
social prestige and power) becomes more, and not less,
intense. "Welfare for everybody, status for me" is an
increasingly common creed. And in a society without
religious inspiration it is hard to see how it could be
otherwise. Men must have some objective in life, and
equal status for everybody (when one remembers that
status means power and prestige, whose essence is
inequality) doesn't make sense.

The yearning for status is one aspect of a psychological need of which another aspect is the appeal of social
"solidarity." In the first case the ego is comforted by
the sense of being set apart from the crowd and

"warmly wrapped in social consideration," [5] and in the second case it acquires a sense of warmth and comfort by submerging itself in the crowd. And the two methods can also be combined. You battle your way into a group possessing social prestige, and once inside it you enjoy the sense of solidarity of a club member. These phenomena of social psychology are of course not peculiar to the twentieth century; but the more rootless and irreligious the society, the more lonely and unprotected the ego feels and the more desperately it clutches at any promise of comfort and warmth.

In such a society the last words of the last chapter of *The Need for Roots* have the sound of a voice crying in the wilderness. They are as follows:

> It is not difficult to define the place that physical labour should occupy in a well-ordered social life. It should be its spiritual core.[6]

Time will show whether these words are as irrelevant to the modern world as they may appear. They need, in any case, to be read in the light of Simone Weil's more esoteric thought, which we have not yet examined. But in the meantime there remains to be considered her magisterial exposure of the futility of the modern controversy between religion and science.

She includes the lack of religious inspiration among the four major problems of twentieth century civilisation, so it follows that the modern religion which is in conflict with science is pseudoreligion, just as the science is pseudoscience. But the name of the pseudo-religion which she criticises in the third part of *The Need for Roots* is Christianity, and it is, for the most part, in the name of a true religion also called Christianity that she criticises it. As I have already admitted, a complete clarification of her attitude towards the

Christian church seems impossible. She used the word
catholic sometimes in such a broad sense as to obliter-
ate the distinction between Christianity and any other
genuinely mystical religion, and at other times in a
much more restricted sense than the usual one—as
witness the following passages in her essay, "Forms of
the Implicit Love of God":

> All religions pronounce the name of God in their
> particular language. As a rule it is better for a man to
> name God in his native tongue rather than in one that is
> foreign to him. . . . But in general the relative value of
> the various religions is a very difficult thing to discern, it
> is almost impossible, perhaps quite impossible. For a
> religion is only known from inside. Catholics say this of
> Catholicism, but it is true of all religions. . . . On the
> other hand, in spite of all the varieties of religion which
> exist in Europe and America one might say that in
> principle, directly or indirectly, in a close or distant
> manner, it is the Catholic religion which forms the
> native spiritual background of all men belonging to the
> white races.[7]

As she is writing in *The Need for Roots* about science
and religion primarily in Europe and America, the last
sentence of the quotation seems to me to explain why
it is the Catholic church which is the main target of
her criticism.

"The spirit of truth," she asserts, "is nowadays
almost absent from religion and from science and from
the whole of thought."[8] And she is not using loosely
the expression "spirit of truth." She gives very precise
reasons for preferring it to the more usual "love of
truth," which she calls an incorrect form of expression. Truth, she declares, is not an object of love. It is
not an object at all.

> What one loves is something which exists, which one
> thinks about, and which may therefore be an occasion of
> truth or of error. A truth is always the truth of some-

thing. Truth is the radiance of reality. It is reality and not truth which is the object of love. To desire truth is to desire direct contact with reality. To desire contact with a reality is to love it. We only desire truth in order to be able to love truthfully. We desire to know the truth about what we love. Instead of speaking about love of truth it would be better to speak about a spirit of truth in love.[9]

The spirit of truth, she continues, is identical with that pure and real love which, unlike the love which is chiefly concerned to find means of satisfaction, desires above all to dwell always in the truth, whatever the truth may be, unconditionally. In other words, the spirit of truth is the *energy* of truth, it is truth as an active force. And this active force is pure love. It is therefore impossible that a science which claims to be beyond good and evil and to pursue truth for truth's sake and fact for fact's sake should be inspired by the spirit of truth. For it to be so inspired, the scientist would need to have a conception of the object of his studies which contained something he could love, that is to say, some aspect of the good. But in facts, in force, in matter, when considered in isolation, in themselves, without reference to anything else, there is nothing that a human mind can love.

> It follows that the acquisition of fresh knowledge is not a sufficient stimulant to encourage scientists in their efforts. Other stimulants are needed. To start with, they have the stimulant which is found in the chase, in sport, in a game. One often hears mathematicians comparing their speciality to a game of chess. . . . People who present themselves to the public as the high priests of truth strangely degrade the role they have assumed by comparing themselves to chess-players.[10]

Nor, in reality, is the prestige of such empty slogans as truth for truth's sake, or knowledge for the sake of knowledge, sufficient to impress the public which idolises science. When people try to find in science something that can justify their idolatry, they always end by praising one or other of its applications. But applied science is technique, it is not science itself. Thus, in France, it is usually Pasteur who is held up for admiration.

> He serves as a cloak to the idolatry of science just as Joan of Arc does to nationalist idolatry.
>
> He is chosen because he did a great deal to relieve the physical ills of mankind. But if his intention to succeed in doing this was not the primary motive of his efforts, the fact that he did succeed in doing it must be regarded as a mere coincidence. If that actually was the primary motive, then the admiration owed to him has nothing to do with the greatness of science.[11]

In the second case he is being praised as a philanthropist and not as a scientist, and he is in the same category as, for example, a heroically devoted nurse. He only differs from her by the statistically greater amount of suffering he has alleviated.

The fact is that, according to the present-day conception of science, if you take away its technical applications there is nothing left which can be regarded as good. "Skill at a game similar to chess is something of no value at all. Were it not for its technical applications, no member of the public today would take any interest in science; and if the public didn't take an interest in science, those who follow a scientific career would have to choose another one."[12]

Between authentic religion and authentic science there is not and cannot be any conflict whatsoever. Early Christianity could have become, like the mystery religions of antiquity, the central inspiration behind a strictly authentic science. But in the course of history both the science of Archimedes and the religion of the New Testament have been transformed.

Science was practically in abeyance for about seventeen hundred years, from the Roman conquest of Greece until the Renaissance, and when it revived it was no longer the same. "The spirit of truth can dwell in science on condition that the scientist's incentive is love of the object which forms the stuff of his investigations. That object is the universe in which we live. What is there to love in it, except its beauty? The true definition of science is this: it is the study of the beauty of the world." [13] But the science that was reborn in the sixteenth and seventeenth centuries was an irreligious science, pursuing knowledge for the sake of knowledge and truth for the sake of truth, without reference to beauty or love. It was a science without the spirit of truth.

And during the long sleep of science, from the destruction of Greece until the Renaissance, religion also had been transformed. In the Gospels, alongside the conception of God as the Father, there is also the conception of a divine Providence which is impersonal, with an impersonality almost analogous to a mechanism. "He maketh his sun to rise on the evil and on the good, and sendeth rain on the just and on the unjust." Simone Weil quotes this and other famous passages in which the spiritual life is described in almost mechanistic terms.

> Thus it is the blind impartiality characteristic of inert matter, it is the relentless regularity characterising the order of the world, completely indifferent to men's individual quality, and because of this so frequently accused of injustice—it is that which is held up as a model of perfection to the human soul. It is a conception of so profound a significance that we are not even

today capable of grasping it; contemporary Christianity
has completely lost touch with it.[14]

Why did Christianity lose this conception? At some
point in its history the conception of a personal
Providence became the only permissible one and,
except by a few mystics who were always in danger of
being condemned, the conception of an impersonal
Providence was abandoned. Simone Weil believes that
this change was connected with Christianity's transition to the rank of official Roman religion.

In support of this view she makes a historical survey,
contrasting three different conceptions of sovereignty.
First, the allegiance to a hereditary authority, as, for
example, in ancient Persia or in thirteenth century
Aragon, or to an authority held by convention to be
divinely ordained, as, for example, the abbot's authority in a Benedictine monastery of the best period.
Second, the ancient Roman conception of slaveowner-
ship, which was extended under the Empire so as to
place all the Emperor's subjects in a servile relation to
him. Third, the relation of Jehovah to his people, as set
forth in texts dating from before the exile.

The first conception, she says, is of an unconditional
allegiance to an authority regarded as legitimate; an
allegiance which is paid without any regard for power,
or hope of prosperity or fear of adversity, or possi-
bilities of reward or punishment. There is an example
of it in Lope de Vega's *Estrella de Sevilla* where the
judges pass a judgement contrary to the King's expressed wishes and explain their action by saying to
him: "As subjects we accept your authority in all
things; but as judges we obey only our conscience."

It was a religious respect absolutely free from all idolatry. The same conception of hereditary authority was
applied, below the person of the king, from top to

bottom of the social scale. The whole of public life was thus permeated by the religious virtue of obedience, like the life of a Benedictine monastery of the best period.[15]

Consented obedience of this kind is a totally different thing from the obedience of the slave to the master who owns him as a piece of property, and it is the latter kind of obedience, according to Simone Weil, that was paid to the Roman Emperor and to the traditional Jehovah. The Romans, usually so tolerant, or indifferent, in religious matters, were hostile towards Jehovah because they regarded the Jews as their property and could not tolerate the claim of any other owner, human or divine. It was a dispute between rival slaveowners. "Finally, the Romans, as a matter of prestige and to prove experimentally that they were the masters, practically killed off all the human cattle the ownership of which was in dispute."[16]

When, in the end, the Christian church became the official church of the Roman Empire it was inevitable that Jehovah, now reconciled with Rome, should be turned into a counterpart of the Emperor; and accordingly "the impersonal aspect of God and of divine Providence was thrust into the background."[17] Thus God was conceived as intervening personally in the world to adjust certain means in view of certain particular ends—a conception which implies the admission that the order of the world, if left to itself and without special intervention of God at a particular time and place for a particular purpose might produce effects contrary to the will of God. This conception, she says, is not only ridiculous in itself but is incompatible with true faith; and it is also incompatible with the scientific conception of the world. The same conclusions might be reached by other and perhaps shorter routes; but it seemed necessary to describe the process by which Simone Weil establishes them because it involves some of her most characteristic ideas.

In contrast with the Roman conception of a personal Providence is the New Testament conception, adhered to only by the mystics, of the impersonal Providence which sends sun and rain to the just and the unjust alike. And in contrast with the Roman conception of a slaveowning God with property rights over his slaves is Christ's conception of God's slaves as "men who have longed with all their hearts to give themselves as slaves to God; and although this is a gift which is made on the instant and once for all, they never cease thereafter for a single second from begging God to allow them to remain in slavery." [18] This is incompatible with the Roman conception, because if men were God's property how could they give themselves to him?

But the Roman conception is still current, as is shown by some words of Maritain, which Simone Weil quotes with indignation: "The notion of right is even deeper than that of moral obligation, for God has a sovereign right over his creatures and he has no moral obligation towards them (though he owes it to himself to give them what is required by their nature)." Simone Weil's view of the relative status of obligations and rights naturally makes this opinion odious to her. It is inappropriate, she says, to speak either of obligation or of right in connexion with God. But of the two it is infinitely worse to speak of right, because the notion of right is infinitely further removed from pure good. Rights are mixed with good and evil, because the possession of a right implies the possibility of making a good or a bad use of it, whereas the performance of an obligation is always and unconditionally a good from every point of view. "To ascribe to God sovereign rights without obligations is to turn him into the infinite equivalent of a Roman slave-owner." [19]

Union through love is compatible only with Christ's conception of slavery, of men who voluntarily enslave themselves to the highest good. It is incompatible with the Roman conception of slaves as the property of their master. But the Roman conception of God was necessary for the Church's temporal dominion.

> Consequently, the division of power into spiritual and temporal, to which reference is so often made in connexion with the Middle Ages, is a more complex matter than is supposed. Obedience to the king according to the classic Spanish conception is something infinitely more religious and purer than obedience to a Church armed with an Inquisition and representing a slave-owner conception of God, as was very largely the case in the thirteenth century.[20]

It is quite possible, therefore, she adds, that in thirteenth century Aragon, for example, it was the king who possessed a really spiritual authority and the Church which possessed a really temporal authority.

Bernardin de St. Pierre believed that the marks on melons which suggest division into slices were providentially placed there as an indication that melons are suitable for family meals. All providential interpretations of history without exception, including Bossuet's, according to Simone Weil, are on the same level as this, "equally revolting for the intelligence as for the heart." [21] Nor are the attempts to see Providence at work in private life any better. When lightning falls very close to someone without touching him, it is often said that Providence has saved his life, whereas it never occurs to people who happen to be a mile or more away that they owe their lives to a special intervention on the part of God. So apparently it is thought that God can deflect lightning by an inch but not by a mile, still less prevent it from falling.

This way of thinking would be impossible, says
Simone Weil, if people understood that events are
simply cuttings made by us from the infinite complexity of causal connexions. We make them by
connecting across time certain events with certain
effects produced by them, while ignoring thousands of
others. In reality, one cannot cut out from the continuity of time and space any one event as though it
were an atom; but the inadequacy of human language
obliges us to speak as if we could. The truth is that *all*
events are in conformity with the will of God, and the
divine Providence is not an anomaly or a disturbing
factor in the order of the world but, on the contrary, it
is itself the order of the world, or rather its regulating
principle. "It is eternal Wisdom, unique, extended
over the whole universe in a sovereign network of
relations." [22]

From this point the book's two principal conclusions are directly approached. One of them is essentially the same conclusion that is reached by all
genuine mystics at all times and all places, though it is
not often checked by such rigorously intellectual
methods. The other, which is reached by a less familiar
train of thought, is that all human activities—"com-
mand over men, technical planning, art, science,
philosophy and so on"—are inferior in spiritual significance to physical labour.

We will consider first Simone Weil's approach,
which is essentially Platonic, to the familiar mystical
doctrine. What is sovereign in this world, she says, is
not brute force, which is by nature blind and indeter-
minate; what is sovereign is determinateness, limit.

> Eternal Wisdom imprisons this universe in a system, a
> network of determinations. The universe accepts pas-
> sively. The brute force of matter, which appears to us
> sovereign, is nothing else in reality but perfect obe-
> dience.[23]

This vision of the perfect obedience of all the force and matter in the universe to a system of relations which are immaterial and without any force, she has already described as being what the pure mathematician perceives if he can detach a part of his mind from its servitude to force—which means being detached from earthly needs. It is also the same vision "which pierces our hearts every time we are penetrated by the beauty of the world, . . . which bursts forth in matchless accents of joy in the beautiful and pure parts of the Old Testament, in Greece among the Pythagoreans and all the sages, in China in Lao-tse, in the Hindu scriptures, in the Egyptian fragments." [24] Every visible and palpable force is subject to an invisible limit which it will never transgress. A sea wave mounts higher and higher, but at a certain point, where nevertheless there is nothing but space, it is arrested and compelled to subside. "Thou hast set a bound that they may not pass over; that they turn not again to cover the earth." [25]

This truth shines out even from the very words which Hitler uses to express the contrary error: "In a world where planets and suns follow circular trajectories, where moons revolve around planets, where force rules everywhere as sole master over weakness, which it compels to obey it docilely or else destroys . . ." How, asks Simone Weil, should blind force be able to produce circles? It is not weakness that is docile to force, it is force that is docile to eternal Wisdom. "The Pythagoreans used to say that the universe is constructed out of indeterminateness and the principle that determines, limits, arrests. It is the latter which is always dominant." [26] But, according to the *Timaeus*, it is by a wise form of persuasion that Providence dominates necessity. In other words, it is not by another, stronger force that the blind forces of matter, which we see as necessity, are constrained to obey the eternal Wisdom; it is by love. What causes them to consent to be obedient is love. This was the thought—not only as expressed by Plato, but as generally diffused—which inspired and enraptured antiquity. It was the basis of the Stoic *amor fati*.

In one sense, of course, it is very easy for men to disobey God, or the divine Wisdom. They can refuse to consent to obey. But this does not alter the fact that their bodies and souls are entirely subject to the mechanisms by which physical and psychic matter are absolutely controlled. "The physical and psychic matter in them obeys perfectly; they are perfectly obedient in so far as they are matter, and they are not anything else if they do not possess *nor have any desire for* the supernatural light which alone raises man above matter." [27] [The italics are mine.] Desire is one of the fundamental elements in Simone Weil's system of thought. She conceives it as a universal and identical characteristic of all men, and the key to their salvation. (The analogy between light and the supernatural is also important for her. In the country of the blind a complete system of physics could be constructed, except that light, being weightless, pressureless, impalpable and inedible, could find no place in the system. For the blind it is nonexistent. And yet it cannot be left out; it is what makes plants grow upwards, defying the law of gravity, and it is what ripens fruits and seeds. Light in the country of the blind would be what the supernatural is for us.)

> So long as man submits to having his soul filled with his own thoughts, his personal thoughts, he remains entirely subjected, even in his most secret thoughts, to the compulsion exercised by needs and to the mechanical play of forces. . . . But everything changes so soon as his soul is emptied, through the virtue of true attention,

so as to allow the conceptions of the eternal wisdom to enter in. He then carries within himself the very conceptions to which force is subjected.[28]

Attention is another key word in Simone Weil's system. To learn to pay attention, in her sense of the word, is a lesson in humility. It is not a positive effort of will but a "motionless expectancy," an unremitting, patient, single-minded attentiveness. It is closely related to the desire which prompts it and which, if it is pure, refuses to be satisfied with any temporal substitute for eternal beauty and eternal wisdom.

To the extent that a man's soul becomes emptied of personal concerns and receptive to divine wisdom, the man becomes like a king's son sitting on his father's knee. Although, as a child, he is for the most part under the authority of the king's servants—force, necessity, matter—when he is on his father's knee and identifies himself with him through love, he has a share in his father's authority.

The world can be seen as immutable order, or it can be seen as beauty. The difference is in the kind of attention with which we regard it: whether we try to conceive the necessary relations which compose it, or whether we contemplate its splendour. "It is one and the same thing, which with respect to God is eternal Wisdom; with respect to the universe, perfect obedience; with respect to our love, beauty; with respect to our intelligence, balance of necessary relations; with respect to our flesh, brute force." [29]

I have outlined the major conclusion of Simone Weil's last sustained piece of writing. Does it sound like a complacent one, as certain kinds of mysticism may sometimes do if too succinctly outlined—all's well that ends well, every cloud has a silver lining, and they lived happily ever after, and so on? If so, I have given a very misleading impression of the woman who wrote: "I feel an ever increasing sense of devastation, both in my intellect and in the centre of my heart, at my inability to think with truth at the same time about the affliction of men, the perfection of God, and the link between the two." Whatever else she may have been, she was not complacent.

In the last few pages * of *The Need for Roots* she returns to the problem which obsessed her for so many years, the position of the manual labourer in society; and whether or not the problem, as formulated by her, is becoming obsolescent in our world of automation and cybernetics, her view of the relative value of physical and intellectual labour is sufficiently interesting to be studied for its own sake. (It is also possible, moreover, if it seems difficult to relate it to fashionable contemporary social thought, that it is the fashion that is adrift, and not Simone Weil.) Her view, as usual, has a historical background.

According to Aeschylus, she reminds us, the fire given by Prometheus to mankind was the property of Hephaistus, the blacksmith God; which suggests that the craft of the smith was at one time held sacred. She surmises that there may have been in the very distant past a civilisation in which physical labour was honoured above all other activities, but she observes that in any case no trace of it remains in Homer or Hesiod; though at the beginning of the Greek classical period there still existed a civilisation in which all avocations *except* physical labour were looked upon as sacred, a civilisation in which art, poetry, philosophy, science and politics were all related to religion. But "a century or two later, through a process which is obscure to us, but in which money in any case must have played an

* These pages did not appear in the first edition of the book; they were found separately among Simone Weil's papers after its publication. They were clearly written as part of the book, but perhaps she intended to add to them.

immense role, all these activities had become exclusively profane and divorced from all religious inspiration. The little of religion which remained was relegated to places specially associated with worship. Plato, in his age, was a survival of an already far-distant past." [30]

Under the Romans, not only physical labour but "every human activity without exception" [31] was degraded into something servile. But the so-called Barbarians who succeeded the Romans took Christianity seriously, and by the eleventh century something which might have become a Christian civilisation was beginning to appear, with its principal focus in the countries south of the Loire. We have already noticed Simone Weil's admiration for the civilisation of twelfth century Languedoc. She believed it would have freed itself from all taint of slavery and would have raised the artisans and craftsmen to a central place of honour in society. Machiavelli's description of twelfth century Florence suggests a similar tendency there.

> But a Christian civilisation in which the light of Christianity would have illuminated the whole of life would only have been possible if the Church had abandoned the Roman conception of enslaving people's minds. The relentless and victorious struggle waged by St. Bernard against Abelard shows how very far this was from happening. [32]

And in the early thirteenth century the civilisation of Languedoc was destroyed by the Crusade against the Albigensians, the Inquisition was set up, and religious thought was stifled under the sign of orthodoxy. Henceforward there were two domains: that relating to the welfare of souls, in which there was unconditional subjection of the mind to external authority, and that relating to so-called profane affairs, in which the intelligence remained free. This separation, which has persisted up to the present day, is a fundamental flaw in our civilisation; by preventing the mutual penetration of the religious and the profane, it destroyed Christian chivalry and it made possible the growth of proletarian labouring populations with no recognised place in society corresponding to that of the twelfth century artisans and craftsmen.

This analysis is perfectly consistent with Simone Weil's theory of history; but her conclusion, that physical labour is superior in spiritual significance to any other human activity, is reached by an argument which belongs to what I have called the more esoteric side of her thought. As this will be the subject of the next chapter I will give here only a brief, and perhaps startling, summary of the argument.

It is as follows. To consent to death is the most perfect act of obedience to God that a human being can perform. But this consent cannot be completely real until death is near. It is only abstract, so long as death itself is no more than a remote and abstract idea. But physical labour, although it demands a less violent renunciation, is like a daily death, which some men endure day after day for a whole lifetime. It follows that, immediately next to the full and complete consent to death, "consent to the law which makes work indispensable for the maintenance of life is the most perfect act of obedience which it is given to man to accomplish." [33]

In a well-ordered society, therefore, physical labour should be the spiritual centre of social life.

It is difficult to imagine a more perfect example of a voice crying in the wilderness. But if the twentieth century is a wilderness, then that is how a human voice would sound today.

MY ACCOUNT of Simone Weil's thought, so far, has done little to explain the epigraph to the second part of this book: "Go, love without the help of anything on earth." Simone Weil was constantly emphasising the importance of the many things on earth which are lovable and which can help us to love more intelligently. And so, for that matter, was Blake. So what did he mean when he spoke of loving "without the help of anything on earth"? One could say of Simone Weil that her sole earthly preoccupation was with the problem of creating a society in which men could be happy because there would be much to love in it. And yet she said in almost the same words as Blake that it is man's highest destiny to love without the help of anything on earth. What does it mean?

Simone Weil's essay on "The Love of God and Affliction" [1] gives her answer. It is that the destiny of Prometheus and of Christ is the model of the highest human destiny: to continue to love although totally forsaken and nailed to a rock or a cross. And not merely to love, but to love beyond all reason—like Antigone, who refused to discriminate between her two brothers, the one virtuous and the other criminal, because she was "born to share, not hate, but love." In respect to love, if judged by normal standards, Antigone was an extremist, she was unreasonable. And in respect to love Simone Weil was exactly like Antigone. But we know a great deal more about her opinions than we do about Antigone's, and in other respects they were anything but unreasonable. Far less so than most people's, in fact. What could be more reasonable, for example, than balancing the needs of the human soul in pairs of complementary opposites —honour and punishment, freedom and obedience, and so on? Nevertheless, she must always seem somewhat incomprehensible so long as one's own love is more timid or more sluggish than hers, and therefore more easily persuaded or deceived into accepting stones for bread. But she becomes a little more intelligible if one tries to imagine the combination of extreme love with extreme clearheadedness.

It is also essential, however, to understand her use of the word 'affliction' (*malheur*). It is, like the word 'attention,' one of the key words in her vocabulary, and it belongs especially to her more private or esoteric thought. In a certain sense it would be true to say that it represents one of her obsessions. As she uses it, the word stands for a kind of suffering absolutely distinct from all other sufferings and misfortunes; and it may represent very different things, both in kind and in degree, for different people—what is an affliction for one man not being so for another, and vice versa. But its essence is always the same in that, as soon as it is recognised in its true character of affliction as distinct from any other kind of suffering, it inspires horror and repulsion, and not pity or sympathy; and there is a universal conspiracy of silence about it, which includes the afflicted themselves. It is, in fact, a kind of death, a mutilation or leprosy of the soul; and normal healthy thought recoils from contemplating it in the same way that the flesh recoils from the stark proximity of death.

Nevertheless, there is, according to Simone Weil, a way of enduring it which makes it the greatest privilege and the highest destiny possible for a human being.

Since all this sounds rather morbid, and since critics have accused Simone Weil of a morbid predilection for suffering, it must be made clear that her definition of affliction precludes the possibility of its being voluntarily embraced. By definition, it is a kind of suffering which is fled from and unwillingly endured. And further it must be remembered that Simone Weil believed that joy contains an equivalent potentiality of enlightenment. ("The only two ways are affliction and pure and extreme joy; but affliction is Christ's way.") [2] It is true, nevertheless, that her personal attitude is not quite consistent. Although she said that affliction is suffering that comes unsought she wrote to Maurice Schumann importuning him to get her a mission which she hoped would lead to physical affliction and almost certain death for herself; and she wrote to Father Perrin: "Whenever I think of the crucifixion of Christ I commit the sin of envy." [3] But these inconsistencies do not affect her principle that affliction cannot be voluntarily embraced. (Her eventual death in a comfortable nursing home may have been, for her, all the more of an affliction because it was so different from what she would have chosen.) And in any case her definition of affliction makes it impossible that she could have recommended it for other people. All she could do was to affirm her belief that if it comes and if it is rightly endured it is a key which opens the door to the "other reality" which is the source of all the good that ever comes into this world.

And from another point of view, it would be superfluous to recommend affliction, because death, which is a perfect example of it, comes to everyone anyway. But when Simone Weil uses the word she is generally referring to the afflictions which come before death and which, although they can take many different forms, have all one feature in common; they are as destructive to the ego, to what we call our personality, as death itself. And it is precisely for this reason that they can be a key to the door of the "other reality"; because the condition for access to that reality is the *consented* destruction, or "decreation," of our personality. But on the other hand, to fall into affliction and suffer the destruction of one's personality without consenting to it is utter disaster. It reduces the victim of affliction to a subhuman level.

This raises the question of whether any human help can save a man from being destroyed by affliction. It will be remembered that in her letter to Joë Bousquet Simone Weil describes consolations as positively undesirable, as "evil," for those who are able to profit from affliction; but there are many who cannot profit from it and whom it will destroy if nobody helps them. When a man has fallen into some affliction which has destroyed his self-respect and made him an object of horror in his own eyes, and he is in danger of sinking to a still lower level where he is no longer conscious even of horror but is a piece of walking debris with no more than the outward appearance of a human being, is there any hope for him? Short of a miracle, says Simone Weil, it is impossible to help him, because no normal person will be able to bear even to glance at his affliction, much less to give his whole attention to it.

> A stag advancing voluntarily step by step to offer itself to the teeth of a pack of hounds is about as probable as an act of attention directed towards a real affliction which is close at hand, on the part of a mind which is free to avoid it.
>
> But that which is indispensable to the good and is impossible naturally is always possible supernaturally.[4]

The solution is similar to the solution of the problem of justice. The just man is he who acts contrary to the laws of nature by refraining from the use of all the power at his disposal. In the same way, the man who has learnt how to pay attention is able to go against nature by making contact with a man in affliction.

It is characteristic of Simone Weil that her short but luminous essay on education leads up to this problem. The full title of the essay is "Reflections on the Right Use of School Studies with a View to the Love of God," [5] and it was probably written for Father Perrin, in order to help Catholic students with whom he was in contact. In it she recalls the Curé d'Ars, who was rewarded for his long and unsuccessful attempts to learn Latin by a marvellous gift of discernment into the human soul. This illustrates a universal law, she says. "Never in any case whatever is any effort of genuine attention wasted. It always has an effect in the spiritual sphere and consequently in the lower sphere of the intellect also, because all spiritual light enlightens the mind." But the effect may not appear until long afterwards, and then, as with the Curé d'Ars, in some totally unexpected way. A student who makes a genuine effort of attention in trying to solve a problem in geometry may be no further advanced after an hour, but during every minute of that hour he will be advancing in another mysterious dimension; and perhaps one day, thanks to that fruitless effort, he will be able to perceive more directly the beauty of a line of Racine.

But attention is not a kind of muscular effort of willpower. When a teacher says: "Now pay attention," the students frown and hold their breath and contract their muscles. But what are they paying attention to? Nothing at all. They are simply contracting their muscles. As with scientists, so with students, attention without love is not attention; because the substance of attention is love and humility.

> When we set out to do a piece of work it is necessary to wish to do it correctly, because such a wish is indispensable if there is to be true effort. But underlying this immediate objective our deep purpose should be solely to increase our power of attention with a view to prayer; as, when we write, we draw the shape of a letter on paper, not for the sake of that shape, but for the sake of the idea we want to express.

The substance of attention is love of God, which is the same as love of our neighbour.

> Thus it is true, though paradoxical, that a Latin prose or a problem in geometry, even though they are done wrong, may at some future time—provided only that we have devoted the right kind of effort to them—make us better able to give someone in affliction exactly the help required to save him, at the supreme moment of his need.
>
> For an adolescent who is capable of grasping this truth and generous enough to desire this fruit above all others, school studies could have their fullest spiritual effect, quite apart from any religious belief.

To consent to the destruction of one's personality is, of course, not the same thing as *willing* it, which would be equivalent to willing one's own destruction. What Simone Weil means by consent is not an act of will nor is it a positive effort of obedience or love. The most that a man can do when in affliction is to refrain from ceasing to wish to love. He can choose whether or not to remain oriented towards love. And if he endures to the end he will be saved.

This appears to be the central idea of Simone Weil's essay on affliction. It becomes clearer in the light of another essay which she wrote approximately a year

later, in 1943, on "Human Personality." [6] The theme
of this essay is similar: that the destruction of personality is a precondition for contact between the reality
of this world and the other reality, between the realm
of force and the realm of justice. But the approach is
different and the problem is discussed in relation to
society rather than to the individual. And since personality is generally regarded nowadays as something to be
prized and encouraged, the essay is often misunderstood and disliked. But it may well be that anyone who
has really understood any one part of Simone Weil's
work will understand all the rest of it. The appearance
of fragmentariness is due simply to the fact that she
left behind her little more than a collection of notebooks and essays; but the more closely they are
regarded the more obvious it becomes that they are
inspired by a few perfectly clear, consistent, and
coherent ideas, and in spite of some superficial exag-
gerations and idiosyncratic distortions these ideas can
be recognised, in harmonious combination, as the basis
of every piece of writing she produced. The key to her
essay on personality can be found in her "profession of
faith" in a sentence which I have previously quoted:
"All human beings are absolutely identical in so far as
they can be thought of as consisting of a centre, which
is an unquenchable desire for good, surrounded by an
accretion of psychic and physical matter." The centre
is the only valuable part, and the rest is what makes up
their personality, the thing they call "I." The more our
personality is exalted, the more we tend to identify
ourselves with it, forgetting that there is anything else
in us.

> Whenever we raise up the "I" (the social "I," the
> psychological "I," etc), no matter how high we raise it,
> we degrade ourselves infinitely be reducing the self to
> being no more than that. [7]

On the other hand, when the "I" is humiliated and degraded we know that we are more than that. A beautiful woman seeing herself in a mirror may all too easily think that she is what she sees and forget the shame and degradation of reducing herself to so little. But an ugly woman knows that she is not what she sees.

So we are brought back, as always with Simone Weil, to the longing for perfection, the unquenchable desire for perfect beauty and perfect goodness, which we betray whenever we try to fix it upon anything in this world. What Simone Weil preached was man's vocation of perfection, and anyone who tries to preach this vocation in sane language is bound to fall into contradiction. Only lunatics can be logical; and in saying that Simone Weil's thoughts are consistent and coherent I naturally did not mean to imply that they escape the universal fate of all human thinking. In her case, as we have had several occasions to notice, the most obvious contradiction is this: in some of her political essays and in *The Need for Roots* she appears to believe that man can and ought to be happy and that it may be possible so to organise society as to increase human happiness; but in her religious and philosophical essays, in spite of an occasional reference to joy as a means of salvation, the prevailing idea is that salvation comes only through despair.

Not that the contradiction is absolute. In *The Need for Roots*, for example, which is inspired by the hope of a regenerated France after the war, there is an undertone of tragic realism. She does not forget that in this world "only death is true," [8] and that theories of creative evolution, life force, or *élan vital*, are no more than wishfulfilments. All they prove is that circumstances compel us to believe what it is necessary to believe in order to go on living. ("This servitude has been raised to the rank of a doctrine under the name of pragmatism, and Bergson's philosophy is a form of pragmatism.") [9] And conversely, in the essay on personality, which is more concerned with the tragic aspect of human destiny, she still believes that, although "pure good from heaven only reaches the earth in imperceptible quantities," it can sometimes operate decisively as a catalyst in social affairs.

> Just as the catalysts or bacteria, such as yeast, operate by their mere presence in chemical reactions, so in human affairs the invisible seed of pure good is decisive when it is put in the right place. [10]

But before we can put it in the right place the problem is to know how to detect the invisible seed of pure good; and if I have given in these pages anything like an intelligible account of Simone Weil's thought, the reader will be able by now to forsee with almost mathematical accuracy how she approaches that problem.

In the first place, the only potentially good part of a human being is the impersonal part, the place in his soul where, from birth to death, he "goes on indomitably expecting, in the teeth of all experience of crimes committed, suffered, and witnessed, that good and not evil will be done to him." [11] This point in his soul where he thirsts incessantly for pure good may be very deeply buried in his personality; he may have succeeded in making it imperceptible even to himself, as everyone is strongly tempted to do, for the sake of peace and a quiet life; but it is always there and it always remains, even in the most corrupt of men, perfectly intact and totally innocent.

By a rigorous law of celestial mechanics, anyone who loves truth sufficiently to endure the consequences of loving truth will in the end draw down upon himself a part of the good and it will "shine through him upon

all that surrounds him." [12] It will be remembered that
for Simone Weil the love of truth means the desire to
love truthfully, which means, in the last resort, recognising that everything we value in this world is pre-
carious at best and ultimately doomed. (Beauty is a
fleeting coincidence between chance and the good;
chance being the situation produced at any given time
and place by the blind mechanical working of the laws
of nature.) And it means recognising that all the
comfortable theories, of progress, etc, which seek to
mitigate this fact are false; they are forms of pragmatism and are no more than symptoms of our
enslavement to matter. But clearheadedness of this
kind is likely to lead to despair, and indeed it is
generally through despair, through affliction, that
truth is reached. "A village idiot is as close to truth as a
child prodigy. The one and the other are separated
from it only by a wall. But the only way into truth is
through one's own annihilation; through dwelling a
long time in a state of extreme and total humiliation." [13]

To speak of clearheadedness in connexion with a
village idiot may seem paradoxical. But love of truth,
in Simone Weil's sense, does not call for talent, and
she is not afraid to say that:

> A village idiot in the literal sense of the word, if he really
> loves truth, is infinitely superior to Aristotle in his
> thought, even though he never utters anything but
> inarticulate murmurs. He is infinitely closer to Plato
> than Aristotle ever was. He has genius, while only the
> word talent applies to Aristotle.[14]

Quoted in isolation, this passage may sound preposterous, but to the reader who understands the context
it is not. It emerges from a train of thought which can

be summarised as follows: genius, whether obscure and unrecognised or whether visibly manifested in great works, is always the same; it is "the supernatural virtue of humility in the realm of thought," the virtue whose effect is to place a man in contact with the "other reality," and it calls for the ability to persist in paying attention to that reality even in the depth of affliction. Another of its characteristics is a kind of impersonality or anonymity.

> When science, art, literature, and philosophy are simply the manifestation of personality they are on a level where glorious and dazzling achievements are possible, which can make a man's name live for thousands of years. But above this level, far above, separated by an abyss, is the level where the highest things are achieved. These things are essentially anonymous.
>
> It is pure chance whether the names of those who reach this level are preserved or not; even when they are remembered they have become anonymous. Their personality has vanished.[15]

How much do we know about Jesus as a man? Or about the author of the *Iliad*? Or even about the personality of Shakespeare? As Simone Weil puts it:

> Gregorian chant, Romanesque architecture, the *Iliad*, the invention of geometry were not, for the people through whom they were brought into being and made available to us, occasions for the manifestation of personality.[16]

And when genius is unaccompanied by talent and therefore unexpressed in visible works it may remain totally obscure and unrecognised, unless by a few equally obscure people who come in contact with it. But "in human affairs the invisible seed of pure good is decisive when it is put in the right place" and therefore "idiots, men without talent, men whose talent is average or only a little more, must be encouraged if they possess genius"; [17] and there is no danger of making them proud, because love of truth is always accompanied with humility. "What is needed is to cherish the growth of genius, with a warm and tender respect and not, as the men of 1789 proposed, to encourage the flowering of talents." [18]

Not that talent is unimportant, but it can be counted on to take care of itself, and it brings no light from the world of justice into the world of force and matter (as witness, Aristotle on slavery). And without that illumination human society can only be, in one form or another, a collective animal, a monster controlled by nothing except the blind operation of the laws of social mechanics. It was this kind of monster that Simone Weil saw in the Roman Empire and also in the modern State, whether totalitarian or democratic. The collective animal encourages, either simultaneously or in alternation, the following aberrations: the ideal of false greatness, the struggle for rights and the neglect of obligations, rootlessness, the overvaluation of personality, universal proletarianisation, social solidarity in the sense of group self-righteousness, the confusion of talent with genius, the party spirit, religious and national and racial and class chauvinism, and the idolatry of the State. Such is collective humanity, and here are some of Simone Weil's reflections upon it:

> The human being can only escape from the collective by raising himself above the personal and entering into the impersonal. The moment he does this, there is something in him, a small portion of his soul, upon which nothing of the collective can get a hold. If he can root himself in the impersonal good so as to be able to draw energy from it, then he is in a condition, whenever he feels the obligation to do so, to bring to bear without any outside help, against any collectivity a small but real force.

There are occasions when an almost infinitesimal force can be decisive. A collectivity is much stronger than a single man; but every collectivity depends for its existence upon operations, of which simple addition is the elementary example, which can only be performed by a mind in a state of solitude.

This dependence suggests a method of giving the impersonal a hold on the collective, if only we could find out how to use it.

Every man who has once touched the level of the impersonal is charged with a responsibility towards all human beings: to safeguard, not their persons, but whatever frail potentialities are hidden within them for passing over to the impersonal. . . .

Relations between the collectivity and the person should be arranged with the sole purpose of removing whatever is detrimental to the growth and mysterious germination of the impersonal element in the soul.[19]

As is made abundantly clear in *The Need for Roots*, Simone Weil is no anarchist, and it is not from that point of view that she criticises the collectivity. She believes in order and hierarchy as well as in freedom and equality, but what she wants is a live collectivity instead of a mechanical one governed by blind natural law, a human society instead of a crowd functioning automatically as a collective animal. However, when she says that the man who has touched the level of the impersonal is the only channel through which a little justice, order, legitimacy, and respect for obligations can be instilled into the social mechanism, it is perhaps, in a way, rather too easy to agree with her. Too easy because, while she herself had earned the right to say it, most people are neither willing, nor believe themselves to be able, to earn the same right; and in that case it seems doubtfully honest to claim to agree.

When one reads her descriptions, which are confirmed by the majority of genuine mystics, of the process by which the personality is destroyed, it is almost impossible not to react in one or the other of two ways. Either one admires from a distance, in the conviction that not one man in a million would be able to pay the price of the experience; or else one reacts violently away from the whole conception of impersonality into a defiant assertion of the personal. Against self-contempt, renunciation, passivity, and methodical detachment one asserts self-esteem, wilfulness, intuitive fancy, and love of pleasure. One thinks of D. H. Lawrence, for example, who exclaimed that we ought to give thanks for being alive in the body in this world with all its sensuous marvels.

But the truth is, of course, that this assertion does not contradict Simone Weil, who saw equal efficacity in affliction and in extreme and pure joy, and who said that "full reality for a man, even for a perfect man, lies within this world." [20] It is in fact both psychologically and physically impossible to be self-centred, and the only question is, to what objects outside ourself do we adhere? Therefore, in so far as what is being asserted is the pure joy of life and the pure love of pleasure—and in the case of Lawrence, at any rate, there is no question of impure love or joy—it follows that the assertion is simply another way of approaching the impersonal. For Lawrence, as much as for Simone Weil, the moral is that "we do not belong to ourselves" and that joy is never egoistic but always in a sense impersonal whenever it is complete and pure. Only whereas Simone Weil chose tragedy, without repudiating joy, Lawrence appears to have tried to assert the joy of life *against* tragedy, which he repudiated. But he was obliged to live it, nevertheless.

Lawrence's life is, in fact, a profound commentary

on Simone Weil's thought; and, although these two extraordinary geniuses may appear at first sight antithetical, it would be possible to carry much further the parallel between them which I suggested in an earlier book. The whole of Lawrence's life can be seen as a protest against precisely that condition of western civilisation which Simone Weil described as uprootedness; he uprooted himself in the hope of rediscovering the roots of our civilisation. He tore himself away from England, and then from Europe, and spent his life as an exile, in Australia, in New Mexico, in Mexico, and then in Europe again, where he died in despair. And nearly all the characteristics of modern life which tortured him are discussed by Simone Weil, in *The Need for Roots* and elsewhere, among the evils of deracination: shallow intellectualism, the cult of personality, the degradation of physical labour by the substitution of the cash nexus for the bond of personal loyalty, humanistic progressivism, the worship of a loveless and godless science, and the loss of the sense of the supernatural, the impersonal, the other reality.

Both Simone Weil and Lawrence were political pessimists, as regards not only the immediate but also the comparatively distant future. But Simone Weil's vision is less fevered than Lawrence's. Remembering that all force is subject to an invisible and immaterial limiting factor, she believed that a day must inevitably come when the political tide now driving towards an ever greater centralisation of power in ever larger and more comprehensive social groups will begin to flow the other way. "But I don't think it will happen soon," she wrote, "more likely in a future too distant to be measured in human lives. And I am quite certain that wherever centralisation has once become established it will not disappear before having killed—not temporarily paralysed, but killed—all sorts of precious things whose preservation would have been essential if the next dispensation was to be a living intercourse between diverse and mutually independent centres instead of a dreary chaos." [21]

This bleak vision was unrelieved by anything except her certainty that our world will always contain, even though in infinitesimal quantities, "the invisible seed of pure good," which can sometimes be decisive, and that the supply of it in its own world is inexhaustible.

13 THE NOTEBOOKS

PERHAPS THE WORST LACUNA in the preceding chapters
is the infrequency and inadequacy of the references to
Simone Weil's notebooks, but to do them justice
would require a separate volume. Covering the period
1940–43, they contain, of course, the raw material of
some of her other writings of those years, but they contain much else besides and they reveal, what the severely simple style of her other books is careful to disguise, namely, the enormous range and depth of her
erudition. For the most part, the notebooks are very
readable, and it is tantalising, when one sees how many
ideas—in mathematics, psychology, folklore, and other
fields—were competing for her attention, to think of
the books that have been lost through her early death.

One of them might perhaps have been a critique of
algebra. A frequent topic of the notebooks is her
objection to the type of abstract thinking that is
facilitated by the use of algebraic signs. The problem is
that "our minds are so made that it is only possible
really to reflect upon the particular, while the object of
reflection is essentially the universal"; [1] and the modern solution is by the use of signs representing what is
common to a number of different things. It is a bad
solution, she says, and she keeps asking herself whether
a better one might not be derived from the principle of

analogy. It is essential to bear in mind "the relation between combinations of signs and the real problems posed by nature (this relation *always* consisting in an *analogy*)"; [2] and the algebraic method obscures this relation. It has the same debasing effect in the intellectual sphere as the domination of money in everyday life. The relation of the sign to the thing signified is lost sight of.

These thoughts are based upon a comparison between the earlier and the later work of Descartes and the deleterious effect, in her opinion, of his later work on the subsequent development of mathematics.[3] But her views on Dirac, Heisenberg, Gauss, Schrödinger, etc, could only be discussed by a mathematical commentator.

The notebooks also reveal the profound sources of some of her ideas which appear farfetched as she presents them in her short essays. The essay on the three sons of Noah,[4] for example, in which she claims that the descendants of Ham are spiritually the most enlightened, is seen to be the distillation of wide reading and long reflection upon the history of Mediterranean civilisation. And the many pages of notes on religious myth and folklore in almost every country and period of history show what a loss it is that she never wrote the book she intended on that subject.

In psychology one of her recurrent themes is the subjection of the human psyche to the material laws of nature, to gravity, to entropy, to the "abhorrence of the void"—her point being that it is precisely the *unnatural* act of accepting the void without the help of imaginary consolations that permits supernatural grace to come in and fill it. And there are some painfully clearheaded notes on the effect of affliction upon those who are unable to endure the void and to cooperate or consent in the destruction of their personality. In such

cases, when a man's character appears to have been
ruined there may still sometimes remain an imperceptible flicker of vitality, which can be fanned by
someone who has learnt how to attend with love to
affliction. But when the last flicker has died there is
nothing at all that can be done; and in such cases,
although the victim's character has been destroyed, he
sometimes remains as self-centred as ever—an egotist
without an ego.

> He just lets himself be cared for like dogs and cats which
> accept food, warmth and affection, and like them is
> greedy for as much as he can get. Depending on the
> individual, he either attaches himself like a dog or
> accepts attention with a kind of indifference like a cat.
> He has no scruples about draining all the energy of
> anyone who takes an interest in him.[5]

Unfortunately, she continues, all charitable organisations are in danger of finding that the majority of their
clients are people of this kind.

Without attempting to illustrate the richness and
variety of the notes, I can only select a few aphorisms
which may throw additional light on some of the
points already discussed and which, for this reason and
for another to which I shall return, will give only a very
incomplete impression of the four volumes from which
they are taken.

To begin with, here is a severe *reductio ad absurdum*
of the progressive belief that the worse creates the
better by a process of evolution:

> To recognise something good as being good, and to
> hold that its origin is evil is the sin against the Spirit,
> which is not forgiven.[6]

And two comments on Freud:

Every attachment is of the same nature as sexuality. In that, Freud is right (but only in that).[7]

The whole of the Freudian doctrine is saturated with the very prejudice which he makes it his mission to combat, namely, that everything which is sexual is base.[8]

On compassion:

We have become so flabby that nowadays we think pity is something easy and hardness something difficult and meritorious.[9]

True compassion is a voluntary, consented equivalent of affliction.[10]

Compassion is the recognition of one's own misery in another, the recognition of one's own misery in the affliction of someone else. What makes it pure is the very mechanism in which La Rochefoucauld thought to discern its impurity.[11]

On the prodigal son:

It is to the prodigals—to those who exhaust all their strength in pursuing what seems to them good and who, after their strength has failed, go on impotently desiring—that the memory of their Father's house comes back. If the son had lived economically he would never have thought of returning.[12]

On the good (after a brief introductory note in which she observes that to say that we always want the good is a merely grammatical statement, like saying "we desire the desirable" or "we love the lovable"):

What we really want in an object is not the whole of it, but the good in it. Bread, for example—we don't want it as something which has weight, or is inflammable, etc, but as something nourishing. . . . The good in things becomes exhausted, whereas our hunger for good is never exhausted. When I have eaten a certain quantity of bread, the remainder no longer contains any good for me. But I can never have enough good (never, at any moment); so I look for a different good.

The good was not, therefore, in the bread, but in the relation of appropriateness between the bread and my hunger.

But this relation, too, only contains a good which exhausts itself, for it is a self-annulling relation. The appropriateness between the bread and my hunger consists in repletion, which annuls the appropriateness.

The only thing which never becomes exhausted is my wish for good. Pure and inexhaustible good resides only in this wish itself. All that is necessary is to realise the fact.

Wish solely and unconditionally for the good, whatever it may be, that is to say, no particular object of any kind. Wish for particular objects only conditionally. Wish for life, if it is to be a good, for death, if, etc, ..., for joy, if, etc, ..., for pain, if, etc, ..., and do this while knowing all the time that we don't know what the good is.[13]

The desire for gold is not the same thing as gold; whereas the desire for good is in itself a good.[14]

The desire to become less imperfect does not make a man less imperfect. The desire to become perfect does make a man less imperfect.

It is therefore a fact of experience that perfection is real.[15]

On contradictions:

A Pythagorean idea: good is always defined by the union of opposites. When one commends the opposite of a certain evil, one remains on the level of that evil. Having experienced the opposite, one goes back to the evil.[16]

Either the mind maintains real within itself the simultaneous notion of contraries, or else it is tossed from one contrary to the other by the mechanism of natural compensations. That is what the Gîtâ means by "having passed beyond the aberration produced by the contraries."[17]

Beauty is the manifest appearance of reality. Reality is essentially contradiction. For the real is the obstacle, and for a thinking being the obstacle is contradiction. The beauty in mathematics resides in contradiction. Incommensurability—λόγοι ἄλογοι—was the first splendour of beauty to appear in mathematics.[18]

A truth is the unnameable (ἄλογος) point with reference to which one can order, by putting them in their right place, all possible opinions on a subject.[19]

Object of Zen Buddhism: to reveal how much the essence of existence differs from that of the intelligible.

To find existence actually within the intelligible is better still. The purely intelligible is nothingness. It is thought without an object, for the object is opaque.

Platonic research into the *meaning* of geometry—isn't that an example of a ko an? [20]

For us, what is real is what we are unable to deny and yet which escapes our grasp. All that we grasp is unreal.

We are far better able to grasp Divine Providence in mathematics than in the world of sense. For I can imagine a flowering apple-tree placed in this landscape by God as if it were a bunch of violets placed on my table by my father. Whereas I cannot visualise a relation between e and π in this manner.[21]

)n the void:

Everything is useful, *etiam peccata*. This ought not to be believed too much, because it is a thought that heals bitterness and fills the void, like the belief in immortality or in the providential ordering of events.[22]

The void—when there is nothing outside us to respond to an internal tension.[23]

To suffer evil is the only way to destroy it.

No action destroys evil, but only an apparently useless and perfectly patient suffering of it. . . .

Purity attracts evil, which rushes at it, like moths to a flame, to be destroyed.

Everything has to pass through the fire. But those who

have become flame are at home in the fire. But in order to become fire it is necessary to have passed through hell.[24]

On Jacob:

Isn't it the greatest possible disaster, when you are wrestling with God, not to be beaten? [25]

On art:

In the true portrayal of affliction what projects beauty is the light of justice in the attention of the artist, an attention which beauty makes contagious.[26]

The author of the *Iliad* depicts human life as only a man who loves God can see it. The author of the Book of Joshua depicts it as only a man who does not love God can see it.[27]

It is not difficult to understand the beauty of certain Negro sculptures when one knows that a Negro sorcerer spends seven days in prayer before making a fetish.[28]

Perfect music contains the maximum amount of monotony that is bearable; the least possible amount of change consistent with the maintenance of the attention at the same degree of intensity.[29]

There is one thing which, I believe, the devil cannot do: inspire an artist to paint a picture which, if placed in the cell of a man condemned to strict solitary confinement, would still comfort him after twenty years.

Duration discriminates between the diabolic and the divine.[30]

On Marx:

It is not religion but revolution which is the opium of the people.[31]

On transcendence:

A point is infinitely small, is nothing, in comparison with a volume. And yet there is a point which, if it is supported, abolishes the entire weight of the volume, and it does this simply as a result of its position.

The reason is that this point embodies a relation. A relation between positions is not extended in space; it cannot occupy a space but only a point.

With regard to any order whatsoever, a higher order—therefore something infinitely above it—can only be represented in that order by something infinitely small.[32]

On religions:

We should conceive the identity of the various [religious] traditions, not by reconciling them through what they have in common, but by grasping the essence of what is specific in each. For this essence is one and the same.[33]

To die for God is not a proof of faith in God. To die for an unknown and repulsive convict who is a victim of injustice, that is a proof of faith in God.[34]

Jehovah made the same promises to Israel that the Devil made to Christ.[35]

Just as any syllable or syllables may be, by convention, the name of God, so any piece of matter may, by convention, contain the presence of God. Thus we may, by convention, speak, hear, see, touch, or eat God.[36] *

It is through lack of faith that the sacraments have been hedged round with conditions.

Either this will be changed, or Christianity will perish.

In any case, a new religion is necessary. Either a Christianity so modified as to have become an altogether different thing; or something else.[37]

On the behaviour of psychic matter:

Analogy between the degradation of kinetic energy into heat and the degradation in the imagination of impulses of the soul which cannot be effectively fulfilled. (Resentment against a superior, etc.)

But other impulses of the soul which are fulfilled

* See also "Théorie des sacrements" in *Pensées sans ordre concernant l'amour de Dieu* (Gallimard) and *Letter to a Priest* (Putnam, 1954).

without hindrance belong to the same level of energy (bad temper towards an inferior who cannot answer back); equivalency between licence and constraint, constraint throws us back into the sphere of the imagination, where there is complete licence.[38]

Those who serve a cause are not those who love that cause. They are those who love the life that has to be led in order to serve it—except in the case of the very purest, and they are rare. For the idea of a cause does not furnish the necessary energy for serving it.[39]

Why is it that so soon as a human being shows that he needs another human being, either a little or much, the latter draws back? I have often experienced this, occupying one side or the other of the relationship. *Law of gravity.*[40]

A long-drawn-out affliction kills the desire for deliverance and makes even the thought of it practically unbearable (in my case, applies to headaches, end of 1938)—Why is this? It is because to be delivered (unless one is rewarded by becoming something more than one was before) would make all the affliction one has gone through seem, as it were, useless. At this thought, the years of affliction pile themselves up into a single weight which has no counterweight.[41]

Disgust, in all its forms, is one of the most precious miseries that are given to man as a ladder by which to rise. (My personal share in this favour is a very large one.)[42]

Turn all disgust into self-disgust . . .[43]

On beauty and sensuality:

Desire of the flesh and attraction of beautiful faces. The need we feel to crush, to shatter as against a stone, our own inner impurity against some external and perfect purity. But what is mediocre in us rebels, and needs, in order to save its life, to defile that purity.

To defile is to modify, to touch. Beauty is that which we cannot wish to change. To acquire power over is to defile. To possess is to defile.[44]

I have intentionally included among these extracts some of the harsher expressions of Simone Weil's thought. It is possible, too, that I have, unintentionally, given a rather similar emphasis throughout this book; but if I have done so it hardly matters, because her selfless idealism and her extraordinary capacity for sympathy and pity and self-sacrificing kindness stand out conspicuously in everything that is known about her life. And as for her death, whatever explanation one may give of it will amount in the end to saying that she died of love. My chief concern, therefore, has been to show that her virtues were not offset by any kind of self-deception or sentimentality but were fortified by a heroically realistic clearheadedness.

Both these aspects of her are well illustrated in M. Thibon's selections from the notebooks, which have been published in English under the title *Gravity and Grace*. By carrying his method a little further and relying upon a comparatively small number of Simone Weil's basic conceptions it might be possible to construct a sort of diagram of her thought, into which everything she said on every subject could be fitted; and it would then appear that in spite of the fragmentariness of her work she was an extremely systematic thinker. But such a diagram would of course convey no idea of the richness, colour, variety, and profundity of the material it served to illustrate.

Towards the end of *The Need for Roots* Simone Weil observes that the modern attempt to turn the study of the soul into a science could be successful if certain purely materialistic notions were introduced and were handled with scientific rigour. These would include the notion of psychic matter, conforming like all matter to Lavoisier's axiom "Nothing is lost, nothing is created," so that psychic phenomena, like physical phenomena, are simply modifications in the distribution and quality of energy and are determined by the laws of energetics. In the same way, she says, the attempt to create a social science could be successful if the Platonic notion of society as an enormous collective animal were introduced and if the anatomy, physiology, and natural and conditioned reflexes of the animal, and its capacity for being trained, were minutely and scientifically described. However:

> Both a science of the soul and a social science are quite impossible unless the idea of the supernatural is rigorously defined and introduced into science as a scientific conception, so as to be handled, as such, with the utmost precision.[45]

If it has done nothing else, I hope this book has shown that Simone Weil's own work is a unique and essential contribution towards fulfilling this precondition for a scientific psychology and sociology.

REFERENCES

In the following list of books by Simone Weil the English editions are given only if no American edition of a translation exists. The editions, as listed, are those referred to in the notes with two exceptions: *Gravity and Grace* (London: Routledge, 1952) and *The Notebooks of Simone Weil*, 2 vols. (London: Routledge, 1956). The quotations from published English translations are not always verbally identical. Fuller bibliographical information will be found in Jacques Cabaud, *Simone Weil* (New York: Appleton-Century-Crofts, 1965).

La Pesanteur et la grâce (Paris: Plon, 1948). Translation: *Gravity and Grace* (New York: Putnam, 1952).

L'Enracinement (Paris: Gallimard, 1949). Translation: *The Need for Roots* (New York: Putnam, 1952).

Attente de Dieu (Paris: La Colombe, 1950). Translation: *Waiting for God* (New York: Putman, 1951).

La Connaissance surnaturelle (Paris: Gallimard, 1950).

Intuitions pré-chrétiennes (Paris: La Colombe, 1951). Translation: *Intimations of Christianity* (London: Routledge, 1957), including some material from *La Source Grecque*.

Lettre à un religieux (Paris: Gallimard, 1951). Translation: *Letter to a Priest* (New York: Putnam, 1954).

Cahiers, 3 vols. (Paris: Plon, 1951, 1953, 1956). Translation: *The Notebooks of Simone Weil*, 2 vols. (New York: Putnam, 1956).

La Condition ouvrière (Paris: Gallimard, 1951).

La Source Grecque (Paris: Gallimard, 1953). Translation: Some material included in *Intimations of Christianity* (London: Routledge, 1957).

Oppression et liberté (Paris: Gallimard, 1955). Translation: *Oppression and Liberty* (London: Routledge, 1958).

Venise sauvée (Paris: Gallimard, 1955).

Ecrits de Londres (Paris: Gallimard, 1957). Translation of selections: *Selected Essays, 1934–1943* (London: Oxford, 1962).

Ecrits historiques et politiques (Paris: Gallimard, 1960). Translation of selections: *Selected Essays, 1934–1943* (London: Oxford, 1962).

Pensées sans ordre concernant l'amour de Dieu (Paris: Gallimard, 1962).

Seventy Letters (London: Oxford, 1965). Translation of most of Simone Weil's letters hitherto published in French and a few hitherto unpublished.

NOTES

1—Entre deux guerres

1. *Oppression and Liberty*, p. 119.
2. *Ibid.*, p. 177.

2—Childhood

1. Simone de Beauvoir, *Le Sang des autres* (Paris: Gallimard, 1945).
2. Jean Ballard, *Les Nouvelles littéraires* (Aug. 22, 1963).
3. Maurice Schumann, *Les Nouvelles littéraires* (Aug. 22, 1963).
4. *Selected Essays*, pp. 9–34.
5. *Waiting for God*, pp. 61–83.
6. *Seventy Letters*, p. 140.
7. *Ibid.*
8. *Selected Essays*, p. 219.
9. *Ibid.*, pp. 10, 31.

3—Definition of Freedom

1. *Seventy Letters*, pp. 12–13.
2. Letter to Xavier Vallat, quoted in E. Fleuré, *Simone Weil ouvrière* (Paris: Fernand Lanore, 1955), p. 187.
3. *The Need for Roots*, p. 251.
4. *Seventy Letters*, pp. 72–87.
5. *Ibid.*, pp. 112–26.   6. *Ibid.*, pp. 1–2.
7. *Ibid.*, p. 20.
8. *Oppression and Liberty*, pp. 1–24.
9. *Ibid.*, pp. 37–124.
10. *Ecrits historiques et politiques*, p. 125.
11. *Oppression and Liberty*, p. 85.
12. *Ibid.*, p. 101.   13. *Ibid.*, p. 13.
14. *Ibid.*, p. 104.   15. *Ibid.*, pp. 16–17.

16. *Ibid.*, p. 70.   17. *Ibid.*, pp. 84–85.

18. Fyodor Dostoyevsky, *The Brothers Karamazov*, II, Bk. 5, Ch. 5.

19. *Oppression and Liberty*, p. 86.

4 – The Spirituality of Labour

1. *Oppression and Liberty*, p. 120.
2. *Ibid.*, p. 121.
3. *Gravity and Grace*, p. 232.
4. *The Need for Roots*, p. 96.
5. *Seventy Letters*, pp. 26–30.
6. *Ibid.*, pp. 53–54.   7. *Ibid.*, p. 55.
8. *La Condition ouvrière*, p. 254.
9. *Ecrits historiques et politiques*, p. 336.
10. *Ibid.*, p. 241.   11. *Ibid.*, p. 245.
12. *Ibid.*   13. *Ibid.*, p. 397.
14. *The Need for Roots*, p. 160.
15. *Ibid.*, p. 161.   16. *Ibid.*
17. *Ecrits historiques et politiques*, p. 406–7.
18. *La Condition ouvrière*, pp. 78–80.
19. *Ibid.*, p. 113.
20. *Seventy Letters*, p. 73.
21. *Ibid.*, p. 60.
22. *Ecrits historiques et politiques*, p. 209.

5 – "Amare amabam"

1. *Seventy Letters*, p. 73.
2. *Ibid.*, p. 142.   3. *Ibid.*, p. 139.
4. *Waiting for God*, p. 62.
5. *Ibid.*, p. 67.   6. *Ibid.*
7. *The Notebooks of Simone Weil*, I, p. 190.
8. *Waiting for God*, p. 70.
9. *Selected Essays*, pp. 154–76.
10. *Intimations of Christianity*, pp. 24–55. Also translated by Mary McCarthy (Pendle Hill Pamphlet No. 91, Wallingford, Penn. December, 1956).
11. *Selected Essays*, pp. 89–144.
12. *Venise sauvée*.
13. *Waiting for God*, p. 68.

14. It is implied, however, in the Prologue to *La Connaissance surnaturelle*.

15. *Seventy Letters*, p. 140.

16. *La Connaissance surnaturelle*, p. 223.

17. *Waiting for God*, p. 75.

18. Ibid., pp. 96–97.

6–"Our Daily Bread"

1. *Seventy Letters*, pp. 150–51.

2. Ibid., pp. 121–22.

3. *Intimations of Christianity*, p. 51.

4. Ibid., pp. 53–54.   5. Ibid., p. 55.

6. *Seventy Letters*, p. 15.

7. J.-M. Perrin and G. Thibon, *Simone Weil as We Knew Her* (London: Routledge, 1953) and Introduction to the first edition of *Gravity and Grace*.

8. *Waiting for God*, p. 221.

9. *The Notebooks of Simone Weil*, II, p. 578.

10. Ibid.

11. *Intuitions pré-chrétiennes*, pp. 38–39.

12. *Waiting for God*, p. 166.

13. *La Source Grecque*, p. 114.

14. *Selected Essays*, p. 41.

15. Ibid., p. 50.   16. Ibid., pp. 40–41.

17. *Seventy Letters*, pp. 159–60.

7–Last Days

1. Letter to Xavier Vallat, quoted in E. Fleuré, *Simone Weil ouvrière* (Paris: Fernand Lanore, 1955), pp. 85–89.

2. *Attente de Dieu*, p. 24.

3. *Seventy Letters*, pp. 158–59.

4. Ibid., pp. 161 ff.

5. For example, "A War of Religions," *Selected Essays*, p. 217.

6. *Seventy Letters*, pp. 169–79.

7. Ibid., pp. 155–57.

8. *La Connaissance surnaturelle*, pp. 104–5.

9. *Seventy Letters*, p. 87.

10. Ibid., p. 178.

11. *Gravity and Grace*, p. 84.

12. Raymond Rosenthal, "The Quality of Modern Life," *The New Leader* (April 13, 1964), p. 24.

8—Profession of Faith

1. Raymond Rosenthal, "The Quality of Modern Life," *The New Leader* (April 13, 1964), p. 23.

2. *Oppression and Liberty*, p. 173.

3. *Ibid.*, p. 174.

4. *Selected Essays*, p. 44.

5. *Waiting for God*, p. 147.

6. *Ibid.*, pp. 148–49.

7. *Intuitions pré-chrétiennes*, p. 38.

8. *Selected Essays*, p. 29.

9. *Ibid.*, p. 219.

10. *The Notebooks of Simone Weil*, II, p. 389.

11. *Selected Essays*, p. 226.

12. *Ibid.*, p. 220.

13. *La Connaissance surnaturelle*, p. 109.

14. *Ibid.*

15. *Selected Essays*, p. 215.

16. *Oppression and Liberty*, pp. 167–68.

17. *The Need for Roots*, p. 243.

9—Obligations and Rights

1. *The Notebooks of Simone Weil*, II, p. 537.

2. *Intuitions pré-chrétiennes*, pp. 145–46.

3. *The Need for Roots*, pp. 290–91.

4. *Intuitions pré-chrétiennes*, pp. 154–55.

5. *The Need for Roots*, p. 99.

6. *Ibid.*, p. 123.   7. *Ibid.*, p. 198.   8. *Ibid.*, p. 147.

9. *Ibid.*, p. 3.   10. *Ibid.*   11. *Ibid.*, p. 5.

12. *Ibid.*   13. *Ibid.*, p. 6.   14. *Ibid.*

15. *Ibid.*, p. 15.   16. *Ibid.*, p. 33.   17. *Ibid.*, p. 23.

18. *Ibid.*, p. 24.   19. *Ibid.*, p. 26.   20. *Ibid.*

21. *Intuitions pré-chrétiennes*, p. 140.

22. *The Need for Roots*, pp. 27–28.

23. *Ibid.*, p. 39.   24. *Ibid.*, p. 8.   25. *Ibid.*, p. 43.

26. *Ibid.*, p. 45.   27. *Ibid.*, p. 68.

10 – Greatness – True and False

1. *Selected Essays*, p. 208.
2. *The Need for Roots*, p. 103.
3. *Ibid.*, p. 104.   4. *Ibid.*, p. 111.   5. *Ibid.*
6. *Ibid.*, p. 127.   7. *Ibid.*, pp. 171–72.
8. *Ibid.*, p. 172.   9. *Ibid.*, p. 115.   10. *Ibid.*, p. 219.
11. *Ibid.*, p. 231.   12. *Ibid.*, p. 228.   13. *Ibid.*, p. 229.
14. *Ibid.*   15. *Ibid*
16. *The Notebooks of Simone Weil*, II, p. 615.
17. *The Need for Roots*, p. 230.
18. *Ibid.*, pp. 232–33.   19. *Ibid.*   20. *Ibid.*, p. 234.
21. *Ibid.*, p. 252.   22. *Ibid.*, pp. 234–35.
23. Henri Bremond, *Prière et poésie* (Paris: Grasset, 1926), p. 214.
24. *Selected Essays*, p. 134.
25. *The Need for Roots*, pp. 235–36.
26. *Ibid.*, p. 237.   27. *Ibid.*   28. *Ibid.*, p. 158.

11 – Science – True and False

1. Adolf Hitler, *Mein Kampf* (Munich: Franz Eher, 1933), p. 267.
2. *The Need for Roots*, p. 243.
3. *Ibid.*, p. 240.   4. *Ibid.*, p. 243.
5. *Selected Essays*, p. 17.
6. *The Need for Roots*, p. 302.
7. *Waiting for God*, pp. 182, 183, 186.
8. *The Need for Roots*, p. 261.
9. *Ibid.*, p. 253.   10. *Ibid.*, pp. 254–55.
11. *Ibid.*, p. 260.   12. *Ibid.*, pp. 255–56.
13. *Ibid.*, p. 261.   14. *Ibid.*, p. 263.   15. *Ibid.*, p. 273.
16. *Ibid.*, p. 276.   17. *Ibid.*, p. 271.   18. *Ibid.*, p. 277.
19. *Ibid.*, p. 278.   20. *Ibid.*, pp. 278–79.
21. *Ibid.*, p. 281.   22. *Ibid.*, p. 285.   23. *Ibid.*
24. *Ibid.*   25. Psalm 104:9.
26. *The Need for Roots*, p. 287.
27. *Ibid.*, p. 289.   28. *Ibid.*, p. 291.   29. *Ibid.*, p. 295.
30. *Ibid.*, p. 297.   31. *Ibid.*   32. *Ibid.*, p. 298.
33. *Ibid.*, p. 302.

12 – Personal and Impersonal

1. *Pensées sans ordre concernant l'amour de Dieu*, pp. 85–131. The first half only of this essay has been translated into English in *Waiting for God*.

2. *Intuitions pré-chrétiennes*, p. 168.

3. *Waiting for God*, p. 83.

4. *Selected Essays*, p. 23.

5. *Waiting for God*, pp. 105–16.

6. *Selected Essays*, pp. 9–34.

7. *The Notebooks of Simone Weil*, I, p. 244.

8. *The Need for Roots*, p. 249.

9. *Ibid.*

10. *Selected Essays*, p. 32.

11. *Ibid.*, p. 10.   12. *Ibid.*, p. 220.   13. *Ibid.*, p. 27.

14. *Ibid.*, pp. 24–25.   15. *Ibid.*, p. 13.   16. *Ibid.*

17. *Ibid.*, p. 25.   18. *Ibid.*   19. *Ibid.*, pp. 15–17.

20. *The Notebooks of Simone Weil*, II, p. 374.

21. *Selected Essays*, p. 79.

13 – The Notebooks

1. *La Condition ouvrière*, p. 122.

2. *Ibid.*, p. 123.

3. *The Notebooks of Simone Weil*, II, p. 509.

4. *Waiting for God* (London: Routledge, 1951), pp. 157–69 (not included in the American edition).

5. *The Notebooks of Simone Weil*, II, pp. 338–39.

6. *La Connaissance surnaturelle*, p. 87.

7. *Ibid.*, p. 252.

8. *The Notebooks of Simone Weil*, II, p. 472.

9. *Ibid.*, p. 443.

10. *La Connaissance surnaturelle*, p. 296.

11. *Ibid.*, p. 166.   12. *Ibid.*, p. 168.

13. *The Notebooks of Simone Weil*, II, pp. 490–91.

14. *La Connaissance surnaturelle*, p. 285.

15. *Ibid.*, p. 308.

16. *The Notebooks of Simone Weil*, II, p. 447.

17. *Ibid.*, p. 387.   18. *Ibid.*

19. *The Notebooks of Simone Weil*, I, p. 162.

20. *The Notebooks of Simone Weil*, II, p. 446.
21. *Ibid.*, p. 526.
22. *La Connaissance surnaturelle*, p. 113.
23. *Ibid.*, p. 111.   24. *Ibid.*, p. 176.
25. *The Notebooks of Simone Weil*, II, p. 574.
26. *La Connaissance surnaturelle*, p. 307.
27. *Ibid.*, p. 95.
28. *The Notebooks of Simone Weil*, II, p. 381.
29. *Ibid.*, p. 554.
30. *La Connaissance surnaturelle*, p. 313.
31. *The Notebooks of Simone Weil*, II, p. 596.
32. *Ibid.*, p. 464.   33. *Ibid.*, p. 502.
34. *La Connaissance surnaturelle*, p. 95.
35. *Ibid.*, p. 46.   36. *Ibid.*, p. 267.   37. *Ibid.*, p. 266.
38. *The Notebooks of Simone Weil*, I, p. 193.
39. *The Notebooks of Simone Weil*, II, pp. 562–63.
40. *The Notebooks of Simone Weil*, I, p. 151.
41. *Ibid.*, pp. 139–40.   42. *Ibid.*, p. 301.
43. *Ibid.*, p. 302.
44. *The Notebooks of Simone Weil*, II, p. 637.
45. *The Need for Roots*, pp. 294–95.

INDEX